fP

Sex, Lies, and Handwriting

~

*A Top Expert Reveals the Secrets
Hidden in Your Handwriting*

MICHELLE DRESBOLD

with James Kwalwasser

FREE PRESS
New York   London   Toronto   Sydney

FREE PRESS
A Division of Simon & Schuster, Inc.
1230 Avenue of the Americas
New York, NY 10020

Copyright © 2006 by Michelle Dresbold and James Kwalwasser

All rights reserved, including the right of reproduction in whole
or in part in any form.

FREE PRESS and colophon are trademarks of Simon & Schuster, Inc.

For information about special discounts for bulk purchases,
please contact Simon & Schuster Special Sales:
1-800-456-6798 or business@simonandschuster.com

Manufactured in the United States of America

3   5   7   9   10   8   6   4   2

Library of Congress Control Number: 2006051402

ISBN-13: 978-0-7432-8809-5
ISBN-10: 0-7432-8809-2

This book is dedicated to
Leslie Dresbold, my father,
who gave me the courage to be my own person.

And Maggeeloo,
my sweet little pup that I adored.

And to Jim's beloved father,
Edgar Anshel Kwalwasser.

CONTENTS

INTRODUCTION

I can honestly say, not one time has Dresbold ever been proven wrong in any of our investigations.

Ronald B. Freeman, Commander,
Major Crimes and Homicide Division,
Pittsburgh Police Department, Retired

When I first got a call from Commander Ronald Freeman, my heart started pounding. "Oh, no," I thought, "I knew I should have paid those darn parking tickets!" But Freeman didn't even mention the tickets. He said that he had heard through the grapevine that I could "read" people, and asked me to come in for a chat.

At division headquarters, Commander Freeman had a stack of old case files involving handwriting piled on his desk. For hours, he showed me suicide notes, confessions, threatening letters, and other writing, and asked me questions like: "Is this person male or female? How old? Is the writer violent? Suicidal? Honest or dishonest? Straight or gay? Sane or insane? Smart or stupid? Healthy or sick? Go-getter or lazy bum?" After every answer, he smiled. Although he never said so, this was a test.

I must have passed, because a few days later, I got my first assignment: To profile an UNSUB (police lingo for unidentified subject) from a bank robbery note.

"This is a stick up," the note said. "Put $50's, $20's, $10's in bag."

After scanning the note for a few minutes, I turned to the detective in charge of the case. "You're not gonna find this guy's prints in your files, because he probably never committed a crime before. He's not a hardcore criminal. Under normal circumstances, he'd never rob a bank. But he's feeling really desperate." The detective nodded his head politely, but I could tell that he was skeptical.

A few days later, the bank robber was in police custody. As I had predicted, he was not a hardened criminal. In fact, he had no previous arrest record. He was a 52-year-old bus driver who tearfully confessed that he needed money to pay for his son's liver transplant. "Without the operation my son will die," he said.

One day, a woman walking her dog on Aylesboro Avenue in Pittsburgh found a mysterious note on the sidewalk. Printed in purple crayon were the words: Ples rascu me. Thinking it could be a desperate plea for help, the woman brought the note to a police station.

The detectives wondered if the note was a hoax. It appeared to be the writing of a child, but was it? And did the writer really need to be rescued?

"It's not the writing of an adult pretending to be a child," I told the lead detective. "It was written by a girl between the ages of five and seven. And I see absolutely no signs of stress or danger in the handwriting, so the writer is definitely not a kidnap victim." Then I added, "It's signed Kealsey."

But who was Kealsey? And why did Kealsey write the note? We turned to the news media, hoping that someone might recognize the handwriting, or something in the note, that could help us unravel the mystery.

That night when I turned on the six o'clock news, a reporter was interviewing another handwriting analyst who proclaimed that he could tell from the handwriting that the note's author was in "grave danger."

"What if I'm wrong?" I thought.

The next morning, a man and his daughter walked into the police station. They had seen a photograph of the note in the *Pittsburgh Post-Gazette*. The 6-year-old daughter, Kealsey, timidly stated that she had written the message to her teddy bear. Her father explained that Kealsey often played detective with her teddy. Somehow the note must have blown out the window and landed on the sidewalk.

Many of the anonymous notes I come across in my work are not as innocent as sweet little Kealsey's. Over the last ten years, I've seen everything from anonymous bomb threat notes on bathroom stall doors to anonymous writing carved into the back of a victim. When killers leave handwriting evidence at the scene of the crime, it enables me to provide law enforcement with a profile of the killer, including their personality traits, family background, sexual proclivities, emotional baggage, and motives.

Several years ago, I was working late in my art studio on a painting when the phone rang. It was Commander Freeman. "Hey, Dresbold, we have a murder with a note. Can you get down here?"

I quickly changed from my paint-covered overalls to blue jeans and a sweater. When I got to the address that the Commander had given me, a uniformed officer met me and escorted me past a gauntlet of reporters into the front door of a rundown apartment building.

As I waited in a corridor outside the second floor apartment for the CSI team to finish their work, a burly detective leaned over and asked: "How are you around dead bodies?"

"I don't know," I replied. "I try not to make a habit of being around them."

I hate to admit it, but I have a habit of passing out at the doctor's office waiting for a flu shot. I get a little bit squeamish at the thought of blood. I took a deep breath. "Pretend this is just a movie," I repeated to myself, "It's not blood, it's ketchup. It's only ketchup."

Twenty minutes later I ducked under the yellow tape and followed the Allegheny County coroner, Dr. Cyril Wecht, and Commander Freeman into a bedroom, where a beautiful young woman lay face down on the bed. The 36-year-old waitress had been stabbed repeatedly. Next to her naked body, on the blood-soaked mattress, was a handwritten note.

Though there were only a few words written on the note, there were several traits in the handwriting that stood out. I told Commander Freeman that the note was written by someone who was obsessed about his physique or body image. "He may be a bodybuilder or athlete. Also, do you see how he makes his double s's? They look exactly like the insignia of the Nazi 'SS.' Nazi symbols have a special meaning for him."

The information I had gathered from the bloody note led police to narrow their suspect list to just one: the victim's ex-husband. He was an avid bodybuilder who had a large collection of Nazi memorabilia, but he was never charged with or convicted of the crime.

When I'm not investigating murderers, painting, or fainting at the sight of blood, I write a syndicated column on handwriting,

"The Handwriting Doctor." In the column, I respond to letters from readers using handwriting profiling as my guide. Every year I receive thousands of letters from men and women, young and old, from all over the world.

I'll never forget the reader who mailed me a birthday card she had received from a man she was dating. Patricia, a reader from Guam, asked me if she should continue to see William. I took one look at William's writing and knew the answer. This fellow's handwriting contained a stroke known as the "devil's fork," a pitchfork-like symbol that appears in the handwriting of people who believe that they are possessed by the devil.

Though it's impossible for me to personally answer all the letters I get, I felt compelled to write Patricia back immediately. I told her to change her locks, get a Doberman pinscher, and tell William she had been diagnosed with a rare medical condition that required her to remain celibate for the rest of her life.

A few weeks later, Patricia wrote back. She had hired a private investigator to perform a background check on William. It turned out that William had a criminal record and a history of violence against women. "Michelle, I have to thank you," she wrote. "I am sure that if I had continued to see William, he would have eventually tried to kill me."

You can read some of the most interesting letters in the last section of the book, Let's Get Personal.

One the most frequent questions I get about my work is "How did a nice girl like you get into this business?"

I never planned on becoming a handwriting profiler. After graduating with a degree in art and psychology from the University of Michigan, I tried to make a living as an artist. I painted and worked odd jobs—such as making jewelry and teaching snorkeling—to support myself. One summer, almost as a lark, I took a course in handwriting analysis. I was amazed at how much one could tell about a person through his or her handwriting, and my teachers and classmates were amazed at how quickly I became proficient in the art of personality profiling. It seemed that my artist's eye enabled me to see and recall subtle patterns and variations in handwriting that others missed. Though I knew that I had a special talent for "reading" people, I never imagined that one day I would be considered one of the top criminal handwriting profilers in the United States.

In the beginning, I profiled people for fun. After a few thousand "readings," I started to build a reputation for being astonishingly accurate. Eventually, my skills came to the attention of the Pittsburgh Police Department and the Allegheny County district attorney's office.

In 2000, I was one of only nineteen handwriting experts from across the country selected by the US Secret Service to attend their advanced document examination training program at the Federal Law Enforcement Training Grounds in Glynco, Georgia.

I expected southern Georgia to be hot and sticky, but I didn't know the mosquitoes would be so big and hungry.

One day we were working on a practice case based on an actual Secret Service investigation.

"Do you see any clues in the suspect's writing?" one of the instructors asked.

I raised my hand. "The suspect grew up in a small town in Austria or Germany and moved to the United States when she was a teenager. She probably has two handwriting styles, one she learned in Germany and one she learned in the United States. I'll bet her early handwriting style matches the handwriting on the note."

"You are absolutely right," said the instructor. "She was born and raised in a small town in Austria. She moved to the United States when she was fourteen."

"How in the world did you know all that?" someone asked.

Handwriting profiling is not something you can explain in a sentence or two. It takes years of experience, detailed knowledge of handwriting and psychology, and, perhaps most important, a large amount of good old common sense.

In *Sex, Lies, and Handwriting* I offer you some of my experience and knowledge.

In Part I, you'll attend my fun super-condensed mini course on the basic concepts of handwriting profiling. In no time, you'll be exploring the handwriting of the famous and infamous . . . and discovering what secrets lurk behind their scribbled scripts.

You'll see how a single letter, the personal pronoun I, reveals volumes about a person's family background and inner self. And you'll discover what your own personal pronoun says about you.

In Part II, I'll introduce you to some key danger signs in handwriting. You'll learn the signs of a dirty, rotten scoundrel and a lying, cheating, backstabbing lover. You'll be introduced to some of the most dangerous traits in handwriting, including weapon-shaped letters: shark's teeth, club strokes, and felon's claws. When you see these traits in someone's script, it's time to stop reading and start running!

In Part III, you'll see how the handwriting of liars, perverts, and "evildoers" can provide insight into their backgrounds, psychological needs, and behavior. And you'll use your newfound skills as a handwriting detective to solve some real-life cases.

In Part IV, you'll join me as we examine three cold cases—Jon-Benét Ramsey, Jack the Ripper, and Lizzie Borden—to see if we can determine "whodunit" from the handwriting evidence.

And in Part V, I'll share with you the insights and advice I gave writers, based on their actual handwriting. I'll also show you how to apply common sense and profiling skills to your own situations.

So whether you are looking to develop a deeper understanding of yourself and the people in your life, or you want to learn how to read the danger signs in the writing of liars, perverts, and evildoers, you've picked up the right book!

Sex, Lies, and
Handwriting

PART I

Basic Concepts of Handwriting Profiling
(a Fun Super-Condensed Mini Course)

1

Brainwriting 101

*Handwriting can infallibly show whether it comes
from a person who is noble-minded or from one who
is vulgar.*

Confucius

Have you ever looked at a person and thought:

He looks honest . . .

She seems friendly . . .

He doesn't look like a serial killer . . .

Are you always right?

The truth is, appearances can be deceiving, but handwriting never lies.

Handwriting analysis is an amazingly accurate tool. It reveals how a writer thinks, feels, and acts. In fact, handwriting analysis is so accurate that the FBI, CIA, and Mossad (Israel's intelligence agency) use it to build detailed psychological profiles of some of the world's most dangerous individuals.

Now, you may be thinking, "How is it possible to tell so much from handwriting? After all, handwriting comes from the hand, not the brain. Right?"

Wrong!!!

Actually, your hand plays a very minor role in handwriting. If you injured your hand and had to learn to write with a pen in your

3

mouth or between your toes, eventually you would produce almost the same handwriting that you produced before your injury. However, if your brain were injured, you would lose much of your writing ability. It is your brain—not your hand, foot, or mouth—that decides the size, shape, and slant of your handwriting. Handwriting is really "brainwriting," and the marks you place on the paper are your "brain prints."

Reading and interpreting brain prints requires logic and knowledge. It takes many years of study and practice to become a top-notch handwriting profiler. However, I bet you'll be surprised to discover how much you already know about handwriting and personality.

To prove it, here's a little quiz. Below, you'll find six pairs of brain prints and questions about the writers. Answer the questions using your good old common sense.

Brain Print Quiz

Question 1. Look at the signatures of two men, both named Ted. Which Ted is the recluse, A or B?

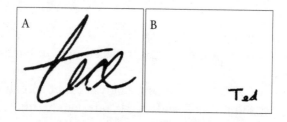

Question 2. Here are handwriting samples of two famous artists. One is feeling upbeat, while the other is feeling down in the dumps. Which artist is feeling down, A or B?

Question 3. Which of these two politicians doesn't want you to be able to "read" him, A or B?

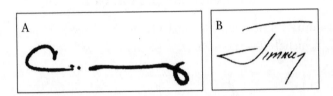

Question 4. Which one of these writers is more nurturing, A or B?

Question 5. Which of these writers holds back when it comes to expressing emotions, A or B?

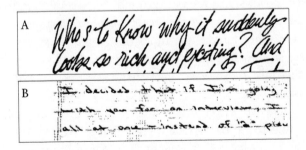

Question 6. Which of these writers is the transvestite?

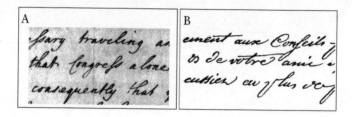

Ready to see how you did?

Answers to Brain Print Quiz

Question 1. Look at the signatures of two men, both named Ted. Which Ted is the recluse, A or B?

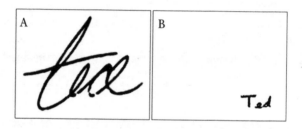

If you guessed B, bravo!

Yes, size does matter—at least, when it comes to handwriting! Is a writer who signs his name in teeny-weeny letters someone who wants to be noticed? Or is he more likely to be the kind of guy who shrinks into the background? Very small handwriting, like that of B, means that the writer is an introvert.

On the other hand, nine times out of ten, large writers are extroverts. They like being around people, they like to talk, and when they talk, they use expansive hand gestures and exaggerated expressions.

The reclusive writer B is a former math professor who sent mail bombs to "stinking technophiles" and "oversocialized leftists" (as he described his enemies in a rambling manifesto), wounding twenty-three people and killing three. When he was arrested in April 1996, authorities found him living as a hermit in

EXPERIMENT

Try this experiment:

1. Get out a piece of paper and a pen.
2. Write your name very large.
3. Now, write it smaller.
4. Now, write it even smaller.
5. One last time, write it as teensy-weensy as you can.

Did you feel more restricted when you wrote your name large, or when you wrote it itsy-bitsy?

a one-room shack outside Lincoln, Montana. Writer B is the Unabomber, Ted Kaczynski.

In the 1970s, writer A traveled across the country, posing as a graduate student. He often hung around college campuses, socializing, playing tennis, and murdering young women. Writer A was outgoing and liked to be around people. And he sure didn't like to be confined, twice escaping from jail. The large signature belongs to Ted Bundy.

Question 2. Here are handwriting samples of two famous artists. One is feeling upbeat, while the other is feeling down in the dumps. Which artist is feeling down, A or B?

The answer is Artist A.

Reading people through their handwriting is a lot like reading body language. If you see a woman walking with her head down and her shoulders slouched, you can sense that she feels the weight of the world on her back. If you see a woman walking with her head held high, chin up, and a bounce in her step, you can sense that her mood is buoyant and bright.

Do you see how the handwriting of Artist A travels downhill? Downhill writing shows that the writer is feeling blue. His spirits are sinking. The uphill writing of Artist B indicates that he's feeling upbeat and energetic. His spirits are soaring.

Artist A, the downhill writer, sold only one painting in his lifetime. Sadly, he took his own life at the age of thirty-seven. Now, more than a hundred years later, his works are considered priceless, and he is revered as one of the greatest painters of all time. This downhill writer signed his paintings: Vincent.

The uphill writer, Artist B, was one of the most prolific and financially successful artists who ever put paint to a canvas. Productive well into his nineties, this uphill writer signed his works: Picasso.

Question 3. Which of these two politicians doesn't want you to be able to "read" him, A or B?

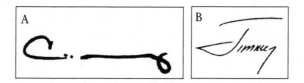

If you guessed A, the politician with the unreadable writing, you're right again.

The reason you can't read this politician's signature is that he doesn't want you to read his signature . . . or him! Illegible scribbles say "Try as you might, you won't get a darn thing out of me!"

Who is this politico incognito? It's Gary Condit, the former

BONUS QUESTION

Here's a bonus question. For extra credit, let's test your understanding of relationship dynamics. Sally's handwriting slopes uphill. Sam's handwriting slopes downhill. Sally and Sam begin working together on a project. Day after day, they work side-by-side in a small office. Six months pass. How is their handwriting likely to change?

A. No changes. Sam's and Sally's handwriting will stay the same.

B. Sam's and Sally's handwriting will both become level.

C. Sam's handwriting will stay the same. Sally's handwriting will start to fall.

D. Sally's handwriting will stay the same and Sam's handwriting will begin to rise.

If you guessed C, give yourself a star. It's far easier to pull someone down than push someone up. Anyone who's been married to a downhill writer for any length of time will know what I mean.

So if you happen to work or live with a downhill writer, watch out for changes in your own writing—and if you see a change for the worse, make a conscious effort to keep your writing and your mood up.

If you happen to be a downhill writer yourself, do yourself a favor: Force yourself to write uphill and think upbeat. If you can change your handwriting, you can change your life!

congressman from California, who stonewalled Washington, DC police and the American public for months about his relationship with a missing government intern named Chandra Levy.

Legible writing, on the other hand, shows that the writer wants to be understood and communicate clearly. Politician B's readable script says "I'm an open book."

The highly legible handwriting of sample B belongs to a plain-spoken peanut farmer from Plains, Georgia who became the thirty-ninth president of the United States. Jimmy Carter received the Nobel Peace Prize for his tireless work communicating his simple and clear message of peace, political fairness, and humanitarianism throughout the world.

Question 4. Which one of these writers is more nurturing, A or B?

The answer is A.

Notice how A's writing looks round compared to the angular script of B. A gentle, nonaggressive nature allows a writer's muscles to relax and create curves.

Notice that Writer B's handwriting has absolutely no curves—even the loops are made with sharp angles. When writers are feeling angry, determined, fearful, competitive, or challenged, their muscles tighten. So a writer who's driven, aggressive, or hostile can only create angles, not curves.

Writer A was a gentle woman who dedicated her life to nurturing and healing the poorest of the poor. People around the world knew her simply as Mother Teresa.

Writer B was a torturer and mass murderer driven by an obsession with "racial purity." This is the writing of Heinrich Himmler, who headed Hitler's Gestapo and directed Germany's systematic extermination of 6 million Jews during World War II.

EXERCISE

Get out your pen and a blank sheet of paper.
Fill the top half of the sheet with sharp, angular, zigzag lines.

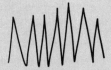

Fill the bottom half of the sheet with curvy, spiraling lines.

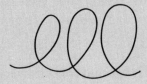

Did you feel more aggressive writing sharp angles or curves? The answer is in the paper itself. Turn your paper over and run your fingers across the surface. You should be able to read your aggression on the back side of the sheet. Can you feel a difference between the two? I'll bet you find that you applied far greater pressure on the top half (when making angles) than on the bottom half (when making spirals).

Question 5. Which of these writers holds back when it comes to expressing emotions, A or B?

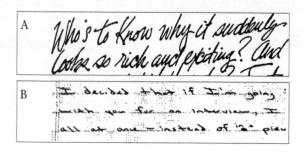

The answer is B.

Do you see how B's handwriting leans back, toward the left? Back-slanted writers lean over backwards to avoid letting you know anything about them.

On the other hand, right-slanted writers lean toward people. Their actions and reactions are based mainly on feelings, and they often have trouble holding back their emotions.

Throughout his life, writer B showed little of his true feelings to others. In high school, his sarcastic classmates voted him "Most Talkative Senior" because he hardly said a word. Ten years later, this back-slanted writer was in the national spotlight, on trial for setting the bomb that killed 168 people and injured more than 500 at the Oklahoma City Federal Building. In the courtroom, he appeared calm, relaxed, and unconcerned. He went to his death stone-faced and silent. Timothy McVeigh expressed no regrets and no remorse for his actions.

Writer A had no trouble expressing how she felt when an officer gave her a ticket for an expired license plate on her Rolls-Royce. She simply slapped him! As for smacking the officer, she explained, "I have a Hungarian temper."

At her trial, writer A was outspoken and feisty. The judge sentenced her to work 120 hours at a shelter for poor senior citizens. However, after working fifty hours at the shelter, she decided to relocate the soup kitchen to her Beverly Hills mansion.

Serving goulash in a dingy kitchen just didn't seem right for this right-slanted writer, Hollywood celebrity, actress, and eight-time bride, Zsa Zsa Gabor.

Question 6. Now, take another look at the sixth pair of brain prints. Who likes to dress up in women's underwear, A or B?

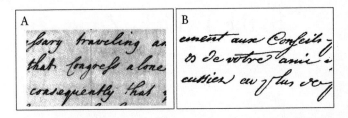

Not so easy, is it?

To learn who's the transvestite—and almost everything else you need to know about sex, lies, and handwriting—read on!

2

From the Erogenous Zone
to the Twilight Zone

Imagine you've been transported into the parallel universe known as CBS Television Studios, Hollywood. There, on a giant sound stage built around an artificial lagoon, the second assistant director tells you to hurry into a rubber dinghy, just as a technician begins to push the dinghy into the water with a long wooden pole.

In this episode, your character has joined an expedition to the South Pacific to rescue the survivors of a shipwreck. On the shore of an uncharted desert isle, you find the tiny SS *Minnow* run aground. Out of the thick jungle, the first mate, the skipper, and a millionaire and his wife run to greet you. The first mate slips on a banana peel, dusts himself off, and then a coconut falls on his head. A little dazed, he tells you that the movie star, the professor, and Mary Ann are missing.

Three bottles have washed up onto the beach. Each bottle contains a handwritten message with a different script and a different tale to tell. For example, one writer describes a life with "no phones," "no lights," "no motor cars," and "not a single luxury. . . ." Interestingly, each tale ends with disparaging remarks about someone named Gilligan.

Here are samples of handwriting from each bottle.

A

B

C

Can you match the handwriting samples above with the cast-aways?

1. Mary Ann, the lovable girl next door
2. Roy, the brainy professor
3. Ginger, the Hollywood hottie

Here are some clues:

- Notice that each of these three "Gilligans" looks quite different, revealing fundamental differences in the castaways' personalities and thinking processes.
- If you were to draw conclusions from the "body" of their handwriting, you might say that one "Gilligan" emphasizes the head, one emphasizes the middle of the body, and one emphasizes the body below the belt.

What is it about each castaway's handwriting that gives them away? The answer is in the "zones":

- The Professor (C) writes from his head. His "Gilligan" emphasizes the upper zone.
- Mary Ann (A) writes from her heart. Her "Gilligan" emphasizes the middle zone.

- Ginger (B) writes from a different place. Her "Gilligan" emphasizes the lower zone.

The Zoning Laws

The **upper zone** contains the tops of the capital letters and the upper loops, or upward extensions, of the lowercase letters *b*, *d*, *f*, *h*, *k*, *l*, and *t*. The **middle zone** is where you'll find the lowercase letters *a*, *c*, *e*, *i*, *m*, *n*, *o*, *r*, *s*, *u*, *v*, *w*, and *x*. All the letters in the English alphabet, capital and lower case, travel through the middle zone. And in the **lower zone,** you'll find the lower loops or lower extensions of the letters *f*, *g*, *j*, *p*, *q*, *y*, and *z*.

The **upper zone** correlates with the head. What goes on in your head? You think. You fantasize. You imagine. You hope. The upper zone represents your ideas, dreams, and thinking processes. The farther you extend your upper loops from the baseline, the more you are willing to move from the known to the unknown, from the concrete to the abstract.

Dominant upper zone: When the upper zone is dominant, as in the Professor's script, the writer lives in the world of ideas.

The **middle zone** correlates with the middle of the body. What goes on in your midsection? Your heart, lungs, and other internal organs are working nonstop to keep you alive. Your middle zone is all about living in the here and now. It tells about your social and practical needs, how you feel and react "in your gut," and how you communicate with others in your day-to-day relationships.

Most adolescent girls are middle-zone–dominant writers. They're not thinking, "How am I going to save the world?" They're thinking about those everyday crucial concerns like "Am I pretty? I think I just got a zit. How's my hair? Oh . . . he's sooo cute. Want to go to the mall?" The same is true of adults whose lives are focused on home and family. These homebodies, like Mary Ann, are emotionally focused on themselves and their social interactions. Usually, as a writer matures the middle zone will recede somewhat in size.

Oh Gilligan, sometimes you're such a pest!

Dominant middle zone: Middle-zone–dominant writers like Mary Ann are social creatures whose lives are centered on the here and now.

The **lower zone** correlates with the lower body. What goes on in your lower body? You walk. You run. You dance. And you make love. The lower zone represents your physical, material, and sexual needs, urges, and appetites. It reveals how you feel about sex and your body.

Oh Gilligan . . . Oh Gilligan!

Dominant lower zone: When you see writing with a dominant lower zone, like Ginger the Movie Star's, it's a sign of a writer with an oversized need for material, physical, or sexual gratification.

Golly, Golly, Golly

If you want to know where a writer really lives, you've got to know how to apply the zoning laws. So get out your #2 pencil, roll up your sleeves, and get ready to take "the golly test."

Question 1: You have just arrived at the final exam for your "Advanced Theory of Twentieth Century Linguistics" class, only to realize that it is based entirely on the one required book you never got around to reading. Subtly, you peer over to the essay questions that two other students are furiously composing. You notice that students A and B each have a distinct way of writing the word "golly." You desperately need some "inspiration."

Who is more inspiring, A or B?

A   B

Answer: B. (Not that you would ever cheat!)

Question 2: You are a detective. You have just been given an undercover assignment: to determine who has been threatening to sabotage the senior prom at Riverdale High. To carry out your task, you must infiltrate the high school and become part of the prom committee. It is very important that you blend in with the rest of the teenage girls. To do this you must have someone coach you on the latest in teenage trends—the hairstyles, the most up-to-date fashions, and of course, the lingo. Here is the word "golly" written by two potential coaches. Which candidate is most likely to steer you correctly on what's "hip" right now, A or B?

Answer: A.

Question 3: *You recently met a handsome Frenchman. He wants to fly you to Paris for the weekend. You are looking forward to an intimate getaway. This is how your would-be lover writes the word "golly." What should you do?*

Answer: Bring along a good book!

Zones Out of Whack

Study the handwriting of a healthy, well-balanced adult, and you'll typically find a script that is well formed and evenly balanced. In balanced writing, the middle zone is more or less half the height of the upper and lower zones, which are roughly equal in height. When one zone is a little "out of whack," it isn't necessarily a bad thing . . . up to a point. But beyond that point?

When does a person with a dominant lower zone become a sexaholic? When does a centered homebody with a dominant middle zone become a person who is selfish and self-centered? And when does a dreamer with a dominant upper zone enter the Twilight Zone?

Next Stop, the Twilight Zone

Writers with a puffed up or inflated upper zone like to embellish and brag. A writer with extremely exaggerated upper loops is often delusional or paranoid.

Life Is Stranger than Science Fiction

These signatures belong to one of the most successful writers of all time. Look at his ballooned upper loops.

Love,

RON

L. RON HUBBARD

Down to his last dollar in 1950, struggling science fiction writer L. Ron Hubbard hit the jackpot with *Dianetics: The Modern Science of Mental Health*. The book became an instant best seller and is still the most popular self-help book of all time, with more than 17 million copies sold.

In 1954, Hubbard declared that Scientology was a religion, protecting his income from book publishing and seminars from the Internal Revenue Service (until Scientology's tax-free status was revoked). Hubbard's followers include Tom Cruise, John Travolta, Kirstie Alley, Lisa Marie Presley, and Nancy Cartwright (the voice of Bart Simpson).

Hubbard's upper loops are exceptionally wide and puffy, typical of a braggart who stretches the truth to fit his inflated self-image. For example, Hubbard claimed to be a "civil engineer and a PhD in mathematics"—a bit of a stretch for a borderline D student who dropped out of college after his first year. He invented a glorious past for himself. "Commodore" Hubbard was a "war hero" with a chest full of fake medals to prove it. In fact, Hubbard, who served in the US Navy between 1941 and 1945, never saw combat and was relieved of his naval command for incompetence.

As for delusional thinking—in Hubbard's mind, his little self-help book, *Dianetics*, was a discovery that was destined to have more impact on the world than "the invention of the wheel, the control of fire, the development of mathematics."

Hubbard was famous for his bizarre, paranoid, and vindictive behavior. US government files contain many interesting letters from L. Ron Hubbard. Once he wrote the FBI to report that his wife had stabbed him in the heart with a syringe while he was sleeping. After a while, Hubbard's letters were ignored, unopened and unanswered. One agent noted in his FBI file: "appears mental."

Hubbard claimed to have an amazing ability to travel through time and space. Here's what he wrote in a Scientology bulletin about his travels to the kingdom of heaven:

- Of his first visit, some 43 trillion years ago, he beamed: "Well, I have been to heaven . . . It was complete with gates, angels and plaster saints—and electronic implantation equipment."
- Of his second visit, a trillion years later, he complained that heaven had become "shabby." "The vegetation is gone. The pillars are scruffy. The saints have vanished. So have the angels. A sign on one side (the left as you enter) says: 'this is Heaven.' The right has a sign 'Hell' with an arrow . . ."

L. Ron Hubbard passed away on January 24, 1986. I wonder—after forty-two trillion years, do you think he remembered to turn left?

Ralph Nader, Caped Crusader

Consumer crusader Ralph Nader was a candidate in the 2000 and 2004 Presidential elections. After his first run for President, many Democrats blamed Nader for their loss. Why did Nader run? The disproportionately tall upper loops in this Nader signature from the 1990s show a man who values principled ideas over practical results.

Nader wrote the second signature in 2004. Do you see the break in the upper zone? Often you will see gaps in a writer's upper zone during periods of increased stress or severe anxiety.

Hypochondriacs and neurotics tend to have lots of gaps or cracks in their upper zone. According to his former editor David Sanford, Ralph Nader is a hypochondriac who declines dinner invitations from cat owners because he thinks cats cause leukemia. Nader hates dogs, too. Sounds like this caped crusader is a nervous-wreckie-poo.

Centered . . . or Self-Centered?

A middle zone that is well proportioned (approximately half the height of the upper and lower zones) is a sign of a writer who is centered. On the other hand, you'll find that writers with under-developed or illegible middle zones are usually not very good with the everyday details of life. When the middle zone is overly large, the writer has a tendency to be childlike and self-centered. These writers enjoy being the center of attention. It is difficult for them to delay gratification. What they see is what they want . . . today . . . this minute . . . right now!

The Schoolteacher

In 1996, Mary Kay Letourneau, a married 35-year old elementary school teacher and mother of four, admitted to a Seattle court that she had engaged in a sexual relationship with her sixth-grade student, Vili Fualaau. At the time of her trial for child rape, Mary Kay was pregnant with Vili's baby. Judge Linda Lau granted her a lenient six-month prison sentence on the condition that she would have no further contact with Vili. The judged warned her that if she violated the no-contact order she would be sent to prison for seven years.

Less than a month after Mary Kay was released from prison, she was caught with Vili in her car. She was rearrested and sentenced to seven and a half years in prison for having sex with a minor. Once again, she announced that she was pregnant with Vili's child.

Why did this intelligent, attractive, well-educated mother of four risk everything to have sex with a 13-year-old boy?

Mary Kay Letourneau wrote the following letter when she found out that her teenage lover was seeing other "girls" while she was serving prison time.

Notice how in Letourneau's writing the middle zone is domi-nant. Compared to her middle zone, her upper and lower loops are stunted. Her dominating middle zone shows that she has trouble delaying gratification. She needs attention and lives for the moment. Mary Kay's philosophy: Act now! Think later!

The Movie Director

Soon-Yi Previn was living with her adoptive mother when Woody Allen, her mother's boyfriend, began taking nude pictures of her. Here is Woody Allen's middle-zone–dominant signature.

Like Mary Kay, Woody married his teenaged sweetheart, and appears to have few regrets about the choices he's made in life. On the eve of his seventieth birthday, Woody told *Vanity Fair* magazine: "I've gained no insight, no mellowing. I would make the same mistakes again." Spoken like a true middle-zone writer, focused on the here and now.

Top Five Questions about the Erogenous Zone

And now, the zone you've all been waiting for . . .
For some reason, people are always asking me questions about the lower zone. Here are the Erogenous Zone Top Five:

5. *What does it mean if a guy's large down there?*
Huge lower loops signify a huge appetite—for physical, sexual, or material gratification. But a huge lower zone does not neces-

sarily mean someone is a good lover. Large loops are about quantity, not quality.

Here's the handwriting of Joseph Smith, the founder of the Latter Day Saints (Mormon Church). Notice the enormous lower loop in the *J* in his name "Joseph," a sign of his oversized libido. In fact, Mr. Smith did like the ladies. He married thirty-three of them.

Smith married Emma Hale in 1827. Six years later, he married his second wife, 16-year-old Fanny Alger, who was working in the Smith household as a maid. Smith later claimed that an angel with a mighty sword came to him and told him take another wife, or die. So he took another, and then another, and another.

The angel would return many times. Smith's brides ranged in age from fourteen to fifty-eight and included five pairs of sisters, a mother and daughter, and eleven women who were already married. Outside of a small circle of family and church elders, only a few in the Mormon community knew of Smith's polygamous marriages.

That was to change in June 1844, when a group of disenchanted followers, claiming that Smith had attempted to steal their wives, published a newspaper critical of Smith. When Smith tried to squash his critics by smashing their printing press and encircling them with Mormon militiamen, his heavy-handed tactics backfired. The governor of Illinois had Smith arrested and jailed. A few days later, an armed mob rushed the jail. Shots were fired. As Smith fell from a second-floor window, he cried out "Oh Lord, My God!" Joseph Smith was dead at the age of thirty-nine.

4. Can you tell if someone's a pervert?

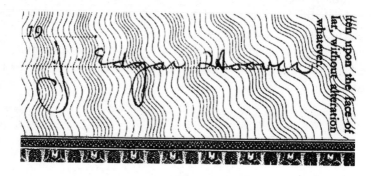

Here's the signature of J. Edgar Hoover, director of the FBI from 1924 until his death in 1972. Like Smith's, Hoover's lower zone is huge. Do you see how the *J* in J. Edgar Hoover's name ends in a coil? Coils in the lower zone show a person who's sneaky and looks for any opportunity to play dirty. Like a snake in the grass, these writers lie in wait . . . waiting for the right opportunity to strike.

J. Edgar Hoover was obsessively secretive about his own past and private life. However, he knew how to use other people's secrets to his advantage. While under the protective coattails of the FBI, Hoover compiled folders on all of America's leading politicians. He blackmailed members of the Washington establishment with irrefutable evidence of their sexual indiscretions.

Hoover's secret files contained nude photographs of Eleanor Roosevelt. (Yikes!) Obsessively interested in the sex lives of Martin Luther King Jr. and the Kennedy brothers, Hoover took their files home at night for bedtime reading. Next to following the peccadilloes of civil rights leaders and politicians, his favorite pastime was listening to surveillance tapes of Marilyn Monroe's Hollywood bungalow.

In *The Secret Life of J. Edgar Hoover,* Anthony Summers claimed that for many years, Hoover was blackmailed by the Mafia, which had evidence that Hoover was a cross-dresser. Summers's source reported that she had once seen Hoover prancing around a New York hotel room in a red dress and black feather boa. This story has become something of an urban legend.

3. Can you tell if a guy is gay?

If he raises his teacup and he extends his pinky finger, could he be gay? Forget the pinky test. Take a look at his lower zone. Do his lower loops (especially on the small letters *g* and *y*) bulge and extend far to the left? This is the signature of composer Peter Tchaikovsky, who apparently had images of dashing young men, not just sugarplums, dancing in his head.

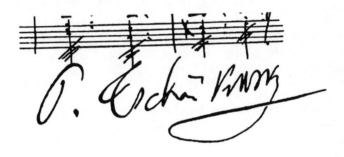

Does he have a flamboyant lower zone? Here's the signature of Elton John:

What's that down there underneath
Elton John's signature?

Finally, is he a flip-flopper, with lower loops that go every which way? If his loops swing both ways, chances are he does too.

Notice the unconventional "flip-flopped" lower loops of the *J*'s in Jim Jones's signature. Jones was the charismatic cult leader notorious for brainwashing hundreds of his followers in Jonestown, Guyana into drinking poison-laced Kool-Aid. Jones once said that having sexual relations with male and female church members was his "personal sacrifice." You'll learn more about Jim Jones in Chapter 10.

2. *Can you tell if writers are sexually compatible?*

The fact is, some couples are well matched sexually . . . and some aren't.

With her strawberry-blond ringlets and her freckled face, Bonnie Parker was exceptionally pretty. Though she stood only four foot eleven and weighed eighty-five pounds, she was hardly a sweet little thing. The sharp and twisted angles in Bonnie's lower zone show she was angry and sexually frustrated. Her hostilities could be expressed in a twisted and explosive way. It has been reported that after she shot a police officer in the head, she said, "Look-a-there, his head just bounced like a rubber ball."

Handwriting of Bonnie Parker

Clyde Chestnut Barrow dropped out of school in the fifth grade and spent countless hours of his youth torturing animals. Clyde met Bonnie in 1930, when he was twenty-one and Bonnie was just nineteen. At the time, Bonnie's husband was serving a fifty-five-year sentence for murder.

Notice that Clyde's lower loops have an unusual assortment of twists and turns. Some loops are squeezed and angular, while some are full and rounded. Some loops go to the left and some go to the right. Some loops are short and some are long. The mixed-up loops in Clyde's lower zone show Clyde was mixed up in the sexual department (which might explain reports that he was attracted to both men and women). And the squeezed and shrunken loops in his lower zone are a sign that he was afraid of sex or felt sexually inadequate.

By comparison, Bonnie's oversized lower loops (especially the huge *J* in Joe's) show that she had an oversized, if unfulfilled, sexual appetite.

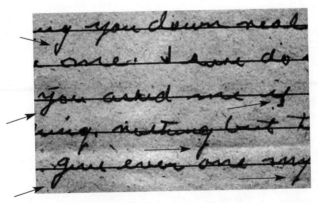

Handwriting of Clyde Barrow

Maybe if there'd been more fireworks in the bedroom instead of on the lam, things would have turned out differently. Instead, in the wee hours of May 23, 1934, along a dusty highway in rural Louisiana, Bonnie and Clyde met their match in a barrage of bullets from a posse of Texas and Louisiana lawmen.

1. Can you tell if someone has problems in the sexual department?

Broken lower loops indicate that a person has had some type of trauma, physical or emotional, relating to their sexual organs, sex life, or lower body. They appear in the handwriting of both sexes. A woman whose lower loops are smooth and connected may suddenly discover gaps and breaks in her lower loops after she's lost the love of her life or has had a hysterectomy.

Whenever people find out that I'm a handwriting expert, the reaction is always the same. "Will you look at my handwriting? Will you do mine?" Usually, I'm happy to take a quick look and say something safe but true, like "you're a perfectionist" or "you're good at sports."

I hesitated when Sam, a man in his mid-forties, showed me his handwriting. "Can you tell anything about me from my writing?" he asked.

"Er, um . . . do you ever have problems . . . being intimate with a woman?" I asked him. He gulped for air and said, "Are you asking me if I'm gay?"

"No, no," I replied, "I just mean . . . do you ever have a problem becoming physically aroused when you're with a woman?"

Sam's face turned red. "Oh my God, how did you know that? I'm so embarrassed. I haven't been able to function since college. It's gotten to a point where I won't even ask a woman out for a date."

Sam's difficulty could be seen in his lower loops, which were broken—split into two separate parts—leaving big gaps at the bottom.

analyze away, tho' your i:
→ was eerily veritable and
2 — now, if you could only f.
number...

I told Sam to see a urologist. A few weeks later, Sam called to thank me. A urologist determined that Sam had a physical condition that was treatable with medication. Sam laughed as he described how the doctor reacted when he had answered the routine question, "Who referred you?"

"You're not going to believe this," Sam had answered. "I was referred by a handwriting expert."

3

The Private I

You can tell a lot from a single letter, especially when that letter is the personal pronoun "I." The *I* is the most significant letter in the English alphabet because it signifies the self. Your *I* reflects how you feel about yourself. For instance, if you feel that you're not up to par, your *I* will be teeny-weeny. If you feel on top of your game, your *I*, like you, will stand proud and tall.

The "I" Test

How well do you really know people? Here are seven "unusual suspects." See if you can match these writers (1–7) to their personal pronouns (A–G) on the next page.

The "Unusual Suspects"

1. Charles Starkweather, a teenager who shot people because they annoyed him
2. Lee Harvey Oswald, assassin of JFK
3. Bill Clinton, American president
4. David Berkowitz, aka serial killer "Son of Sam"
5. Michael Jackson, "King of Pop"
6. Scott Peterson, fertilizer salesman convicted of murdering his pregnant wife
7. Donald Trump, real estate tycoon

The Personal Pronouns

A. An X'ed *I* shows a self-destructive writer:

ʏʼll never forget

B. A bold heavy *I* shows an intense, aggressive writer:

REALLY gREAT AND I

C. A writer with lots of different *I*'s has an identity crisis:

I MUST I cry I live I, I MUST I MUST I was

D. An *I* that's split in two or more parts shows a writer with a disconnected or "split" personality:

I know that I

E. An oversized *I* shows a writer who has delusions of grandeur:

as I am

F. A baby *i* shows a writer who's immature and insecure:

everyday i think

G. An underhanded *I* (which ends on the bottom right of the letter, while a conventional *I* starts there) shows a writer who only pretends to follow the rules:

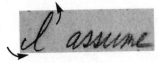

I assume

Answers:

I'll never forget

A. *An X'ed I shows a self-destructive writer.*

Bill Clinton (3)—Clinton's long history of bad-boy behaviors inspired psychotherapist Jerome Levin to write *The Clinton Syndrome: The President and the Self-Destructive Nature of Sexual Addiction.* Clinton recognized the syndrome in himself, writing in his autobiography: "I also came to understand that when I was exhausted, angry, or feeling isolated and alone, I was more vulnerable to making selfish and self-destructive personal mistakes about which I would later be ashamed."

REALLY GREAT AND I

B. *A bold heavy I shows an intense, aggressive writer.*

Donald Trump (7)—After Donald Trump finished first in his class at Wharton School of Finance, he joined the family real estate business. He built a real estate empire and a brand, with his name on everything from condos and casinos to bottled water and vodka. Even bankruptcy didn't put a damper on this self-promoting dealmaker, who, when mounting debt forced his casinos into bankruptcy, declared, "I'm the biggest developer in New York! I have a number one show on television! The Trump brand is so hot, I want to make the casino company as hot as everything else is!"

I must I cry I live I,
I must I must I was

C. *A writer with lots of different I's has an identity crisis.*

Michael Jackson (5)—Notice how Michael Jackson's *I* fluctuates between cursive and printed, large and small. Who is Michael Jackson? Based on his variable personal pronoun, it seems the "King of Pop" asks himself that question every day.

D. *An I that's split in two or more parts shows a writer with a disconnected or "split" personality.*

David Berkowitz (4)—David Berkowitz's personal pronoun shows the disconnect between the two sides of his personality: David and the monster. Berkowitz, of Queens, New York, shot and killed six strangers and seriously injured seven others. At one of the scenes, he left a note: "I am a monster. I am the Son of Sam." At his trial, Berkowitz claimed that he was ordered to kill by 6,000-year-old demons that lived in his neighbor Sam's dog.

E. *An oversized I shows a writer who has delusions of grandeur.*

Lee Harvey Oswald (2)—Was Lee Harvey Oswald a little man in a big conspiracy or a little man who had delusions of grandeur? His oversized *I* tells us he was the latter. "Oswald thought of himself as smarter and better than his contemporaries," writes Gerald Posner. "He was filled with the arrogance that usually only infects teenagers and early twenty-somethings, a self-delusional confidence that the solutions to the world's problems are simple and that he had the right and only answers."

F. *A baby* i *shows a writer who's immature and insecure.*

Charles Starkweather (1)—In 1958, nineteen-year-old Charles Starkweather (aka "Little Red" for his bright red hair) was waiting for his fourteen-year-old girlfriend, Caril Ann Fugate, at her parents' house. When Caril Ann's parents yelled at him to stop playing with their .22 caliber rifle, he shot them both dead. Then, after Caril Ann came home, Little Red went into the bedroom of her 2-year-old sister and choked her to death. Neighbors found a note on the door that warned: "Stay a Way Every Body is Sick with the Flue."

In the week before the young couple was apprehended, Little Red shot and stabbed seven more people because, he said, they were making fun of him.

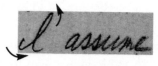

G. *An underhanded* I *(which ends on the bottom right of the letter, while a conventional* I *starts there) shows a writer who only pretends to follow the rules.*

Scott Peterson (6) pretended to be many things, including a devoted husband and father-to-be, a globetrotting entrepreneur, and a grieving widower. Jurors concluded that the real Scott Peterson was a cold-blooded killer who on Christmas Eve murdered his pregnant wife Laci and dumped her body in San Francisco Bay.

So how did you do? Not so easy, was it?

I have a confession to make: I made this *I* test a bit blurry.

Scott Peterson isn't the only writer in our test to make an underhanded *I*. Like Scott Peterson, David Berkowitz pretended to be someone he was not. During the day, he was a law-abiding security guard who said "please," and "thank you," and "yes, ma'am."

Michael Jackson also does a lot of pretending (after all, he lives in Neverland).

The fact that all three fit the description of an underhanded pretender is no coincidence. Look closely, and you'll see that Peterson, Berkowitz, and Jackson all make their *I*'s underhanded:

People and handwriting are often complex. Sometimes, you need to look very closely to catch subtleties in a writer's script.

And then sometimes you'll find handwriting so peculiar . . .

A Most Peculiar *I*

When the *I* is distorted, the writer has a distorted view of himself and life. Writers with very peculiar personal pronouns often exhibit bizarre and compulsive behaviors.

Here is the personal pronoun of Graham Young, a man from St. Albans, England, who liked to describe himself as "your friendly neighborhood Frankenstein."

I am pleased to accept the conditions attached

From 1962 to 1971, no one who crossed Young's path was immune to becoming part of one of his "science projects" . . . not his friends, acquaintances, coworkers, stepmother, father, or sister. After seventy of his co-workers became ill from some mysterious illness and one person died, investigators searched Young's home. There they found poisons, along with a diary.

In the diary, Young kept meticulous notes on each of his "science projects." There were a number of entries about a coworker named Fred Briggs: "F is responding to treatment. He is obstinately difficult. If he survives a third week he will live. I am most annoyed."

About the receptionist, Diana Smart, Young wrote, "Di irritated me yesterday, so I packed her off home with a dose of illness."

Occasionally, he had second thoughts, but they didn't last long. Writing about a delivery man, he lamented: "In a way it seems like a shame to condemn such a likeable man to such a horrible end, but I have made my decision."

Young's penchant for ruining a good cup of tea with a dose of poison earned him the nickname "the Teacup Poisoner."

Someone once asked Young why he became a poisoner. "It grew on me like a drug habit," he said, "except it was not me who was taking the drugs."

Young died in prison at age forty-two. The "official" cause of his death was a heart attack, but unofficially, many believed that the Teacup Poisoner had spiked his own cup of tea.

Mother and Father Reunion

You've seen how the letter *I* reflects a writer's self-image. But there's something even more personal and intimate that you can tell from a writer's *I*. Your *I* can reveal how you were raised, your relationships with your mother and father, and their relationship

with each other. Why? Because your *I* represents you and everything that helped form you . . . including your parents.

Below is the conventional, cursive copybook *I* that you learn to
write in school.

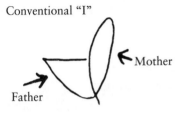

The cursive copybook *I* contains two components, one vertical
and one horizontal. Think of the *I* as a sailboat. The sail, or vertical stroke, represents the mother (or mother figure). The hull of the
boat, or horizontal stroke, represents the father (or father figure).

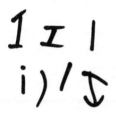

What can you tell from a printed *I*? While printed personal
pronouns share some characteristics with their cursive cousins, it
is generally far more difficult to trace a writer's family background from a printed *I* than it is from a cursive *I*.

Papa Was a Rolling Stone

Eleanor Roosevelt (1884–1962) became first lady of the United
States in 1933. Her work as a humanitarian, diplomat, and social
reformer made her one of the most important and controversial
women of the twentieth century. Let's see what we can learn
about Eleanor Roosevelt by studying her *I*.

If you look very carefully at Eleanor's mother (vertical) stroke, you will see that it is made with two distinct hand movements. The first movement is a sharp little triangular shape. Angles cannot be made when you relax your muscles. They can only be made when you tighten your muscles, for example when you become tense, nervous, fearful, aggressive, or competitive. Extending above this triangular section of the mother stroke is a rigid, straight upward stroke, made with a second, distinct hand movement.

How do you think Eleanor related to her mother? In her autobiography, published in 1937, Eleanor describes her mother, Anna Roosevelt, as the most beautiful women she ever knew. But Anna was also an indifferent, distant, and disapproving mother. Anna expressed her disdain for Eleanor by calling her "Granny," and discussing her concerns about Eleanor's homeliness with her family and friends in front of Eleanor. Anna died of diphtheria when Eleanor was eight years old. Her father was declared unfit to care for her, so after her mother's death, Eleanor lived with her stern and rigid maternal grandmother.

Now look at Eleanor's father (horizontal) stroke. It is incomplete and ends with a noticeable blob of ink. Eleanor's father Elliot Roosevelt was rarely at home. He was an alcoholic who would disappear for days on end while out on his drunken binges. Despite his faults, Eleanor idolized her father. When Anna died, Eleanor wanted to be Elliot's surrogate wife. She wrote, "I did not understand whether my brothers were to be our children or whether that they would be going to school and later be independent." Elliot Roosevelt died from chronic alcohol abuse at the age of thirty-four. Eleanor was ten years old.

Finally, look at the distance between Eleanor's mother and

father strokes. With this large gap, do you think Eleanor believed her parents had a good relationship? Elliot had many adulterous relationships during their marriage, and reportedly fathered a number of children with several other women. Anna Roosevelt had such contempt for Elliot that she forbade him to visit her while she lay dying.

I Spy the I of a Mama's Boy . . .

This is the *I* of Andrew Carnegie, industrialist, philanthropist, and son. When he wrote this he was fifty-one years old. Let's dig a little into Carnegie's history and see how well we can capture his background from just a cursory examination of his *I*.

Notice how Carnegie's mother loop is much bigger than the father loop, indicating that his mother played a much bigger role in his life than his father. Notice, also, how the father loop is incomplete, suggesting an unresolved or incomplete relationship with his father.

William Carnegie, Andrew's father, was a marginal figure in his son's life. A handloom weaver who was put out of business by the rise of the woolen industry in Scotland, William struggled financially through most of his adult life. By the age of fourteen, Andrew, who was working as a telegraph operator, earned more than his father. William slipped further and further into depression and died at the age of fifty-one, a broken man.

Carnegie had a rather complicated relationship with his mother. On the one hand, Margaret Carnegie was his "heroine," as he wrote in his autobiography: "I feel her to be sacred to myself and not for others to know. None could ever really know her—I alone did that."

On the other hand, Margaret was a demanding mistress, driving Andrew from a young age to be the social and financial savior of the Carnegie family. And no matter what Andrew did for her or achieved, it was never enough. Andrew always knew that his younger brother Tom was his mother's favorite.

On first glance, the mother loop looks rounded and soft, indicating that the writer had a soft spot in his heart for his mom. However, if you look closely, you can see that the mother loop isn't a smooth oval, but is slightly angular. This shows that as Carnegie was forming the mother loop, his hand tensed up. So there appears to be some sort of underlying tension in the relationship between mother and son.

Carnegie met Louise Whitfield when he was forty-five. He kept her at a distance for six years. When his mother died in late 1886, Carnegie, the devoted son, was finally free to marry Louise. Carnegie described 1886 as a year that "ended in deep gloom for me. My life as a happy careless young man, with every want looked after was over, I was left alone in the world." Keep in mind that this "careless young man" was a 51-year-old millionaire.

With his large, mostly rounded mother loop, it should come as no surprise that Carnegie was devastated when his mother passed away. But as the subtle angle on the curve of his mother loop shows, while he cared deeply for his mother, a piece of him must have bristled at his mother's control and feared her disapproval. It would have been hard not to feel some resistance to the woman his wife described as "one of the most unpleasant people" she had ever known.

In 1901, Carnegie sold his steel business to J. P. Morgan and became the world's richest man. In his old age, he retired to his mansion in New York and his castle in Dunfermline, Scotland, and applied himself to the task of giving away over $300 million. Mama would have been proud.

All Talk

Dr. Laura Schlessinger, radio talk-show hostess and morality maven to the masses, receives up to 60,000 calls a day from listeners seeking her counsel. She preaches strong family values, and often scolds callers if they don't make every effort to uphold the sanctity of the family. She likes to say she is her "kid's mom."

What does Schlessinger's personal pronoun say about her relationship with her own mom? Here are two different *I*'s, taken from a letter written by Schlessinger in the mid 1990s.

Do you notice that the sail, or mother stroke, is sharp and angular? Remember, angles can only be made when you tighten your muscles. When do you tighten your muscles? You tighten your muscles when you become tense, angry, nervous, fearful, aggressive, or competitive.

It is not surprising after looking at Schlessinger's writing to find out that at the time she wrote this note she hadn't talked to her mother in over sixteen years. Schlessinger's mother, Yolanda, died alone, her body decomposing for months before a concerned neighbor called police. When notified of her mother's death, Laura issued a public statement. "I am horrified," she wrote, "by the tragic circumstances of my mother's death." But then her mother's body lay in the morgue another ten days until Laura made arrangements for the remains to be transferred to Forest Lawn cemetery.

Curiously, Schlessinger's father stroke curves to the left in the first *I*, but curves to the right in the second *I*.

Could this change in direction be because she distanced herself from her father for many years and only reestablished a relationship a few months before he died?

Finally, notice the distance between Schlessinger's mother and father strokes. Laura's parents divorced in 1977. She later described the distance between her mother and father while she was growing up: "I can say that there was little love, affection, and bonding shown in our home."

You're the Profiler

You are a handwriting expert who has been asked to profile a suspect in custody. Your profile could help investigators solve a series of brutal murders by giving them insight into the suspect's personality and background.

You meet with the suspect in a prison conference room. He is serving time for a minor weapons offense. When you ask him to write, he folds his arms across his chest, and refuses to write anything. Then with a wide grin on his face, he says that he will only write one letter. Which letter should you ask him to write?

"How about the letter *I*, as in 'I am Henry'?" you ask.

He grabs the paper and writes the letter *I*. "See what you can make out of that," he says, as he passes the paper back to you.

Henry

What can you tell from Henry's *I*? A lot more than he thinks you can. Here is your challenge. You need to get as much information as you can about Henry from this one letter.

1. First, take a look at Henry's mother stroke. Do you think he had a warm and fuzzy relationship with his mom? Remember, when a writer's muscles tense up, it is difficult to make curves.
2. Now take a look at Henry's father stroke? What does it tell you about his relationship with his father?
3. Who was more dominant, his mother or his father?
4. Did his parents have a close "Ozzie-and-Harriet" relationship?
5. Bonus question: Sometimes you can see the weapon of choice in a suspect's personal pronoun "I" or signature. Weapon-shaped letters, especially when seen in the personal pronoun "I" and/or in a signature, indicate that the writer has hostile impulses and will use weapons and force to rid him- or herself of a perceived enemy. What was Henry's favorite weapon?
6. Super bonus question: For even more extra credit: Name one of Henry's victims.

Reality Check

The man you just interviewed was Henry Lee Lucas, perhaps the most prolific serial killer in American history.

So let's see how much you could ascertain about Lucas based on a single letter, his personal pronoun "I."

1. Do you think Lucas had a warm relationship with his mother?

Do you see that Lucas's mother stroke is extremely sharp and angular? There's no way with a mother stroke that piercing that Lucas had a gentle sweet relationship with his mother. His mother, Viola Dison Wall Lucas, was a sadistic alcoholic and prostitute who abused her son physically and psychologically. She would curl his hair and force him to wear a dress to school. Often, she would make him watch as she serviced her johns. She beat him regularly and ruthlessly—once so severely that she knocked him unconscious for three days.

2. *What does Lucas's* I *tell you about his relationship with his father?*

Notice how Lucas's father stroke is relatively small and insignificant. Lucas's father, Anderson, fell down drunk in front of a freight train and lost both of his legs. Dubbed "No Legs," Anderson sold pencils from his wheelchair. He died of pneumonia, after falling asleep in the snow while intoxicated.

3. *Who was more dominant, his mother or his father?*

Henry's mother, Viola, ruled the roost with an iron fist. Viola constantly abused her husband physically and emotionally.

4. *Did Lucas' parents have an Ozzie-and-Harriet relationship?*

Not by a long shot. Viola forced "No Legs" to watch her from his wheelchair as she preformed sexual favors for customers. She also invited her boyfriend, Bernie, a low-life pimp, to share the four-room shack with the family.

5. *Bonus question: What was our Lucas's weapon of choice?*

Did you notice how Lucas's mother stroke is sharp and angular like a knife or dagger?

6. *Super bonus question: Name one person you think could have been one of Lucas's victims.*

In his late twenties, Henry Lee Lucas stabbed his mother to death in a fit of rage. She was seventy-four years old. Lucas served sixteen years for murdering his mother.

Before his release, Lucas begged authorities not to set him free. Unfortunately, no one listened. Still full of rage and hostility, Lucas traveled across the country, raping and killing. The exact number of his victims is unknown. At one point, he confessed to murdering more than 600 people. Later, he recanted his confessions, claiming that he had made them up to confuse authorities.

Henry Lee Lucas died in his sleep in a Texas prison.

*　　*　　*

I always find it amazing how much a person's handwriting reflects their upbringing and personality. In the case of Henry Lee Lucas, one can trace his grim life—from start to finish—in the strokes of his letter *I*.

4

How to Read a Signature

WATSON: *The man looked like a doctor. Acted like a doctor. Had a diploma on the wall like a doctor. So how did you know he was a fake?*
HOLMES: *Quite elementary, my dear Watson. I could read his signature!*

Whether you're writing a letter or scribbling some random notes on a pad of paper, you are focused on communicating your thoughts, ideas, feelings, and opinions. How you write them— your individual letters, words, sentences, and paragraphs— reveals the way you privately think and feel.

Your signature, however, is different. When you sign your name, you are putting your public self on the page. Your signature shows how you want to be seen by others, how you think others see you, and how you feel about yourself and your position in the world.

Some writers add symbolic images to their signatures, like Ringo's star:

Liberace put his name atop an open grand piano, complete with keys and candelabra.

Charles Manson includes a swastika in his signature.

Manson murdered by ordering others to kill for him. How did this wild-eyed, five foot two man—a man who had spent two thirds of his life behind bars—convince others to commit such horrendous acts?

Do you notice how the swastika, with its four dots and wildly swirling lines, resembles a pinwheel or the spinning wheel that hypnotists use to entrance their subjects? If you stare at it, you may even become a bit dizzy. In his own bizarre way, through his signature Manson reveals one of the secrets of his power. Like a master hypnotist, Manson was an expert at putting susceptible subjects under his spell.

Of course, the symbols in Ringo's, Liberace's and Manson's signatures are consciously drawn. But there are cases were a person subconsciously adds or exaggerates something in their signature, revealing how they secretly view themselves. For example, look at the signature of Joan Crawford.

See how she forms the word "god" at the end of her last name? At home, this screen goddess was a cruel tyrant who forced her daughter to call her "Mommie Dearest" and scrub her travertine floor with a toothbrush.

What You See Ain't What You Get

If your signature is very different from the rest of your writing, then how you think, feel, and act in private and in public can be quite different. Case in point: the King of Rock 'n' Roll, Elvis Aron Presley.

Born in a two-room shack in Tupelo, Mississippi, Elvis shared a bed with his parents until he was twelve. Some say that his unusually close relationship with his mother and strict religious upbringing led to some of Elvis's bizarre sexual hang-ups. Elvis had lots of relationships with both "good girls" and "bad girls" (usually at the same time). Few if any of his relationships were stable or mature. And yet his women adored him.

Elvis Presley's signature is big and showy, reflecting the outgoing, flashy image that Elvis projected onstage.

But the body of Elvis's handwriting is tight and tense, showing that—inwardly—Elvis felt anxious and isolated. In fact, Elvis dreaded being alone so much that he often paid friends just to hang out with him. And while Elvis's signature projects great confidence, his private writing appears small and childlike.

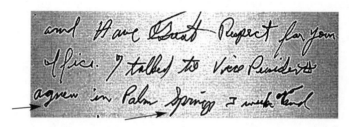

This sample of Elvis's script was taken from his 1970 letter to President Nixon. In the letter, Elvis offered the president his services as a secret agent. He was perfect for the job, he explained, because "the drug culture, the hippie elements, the SDS, Black Panthers, etc. do NOT consider me as their enemy or as they call it The Establishment."

What else was Elvis trying to convey with his signature? Remember the lower zone: the bottom loops of the letters *f*, *g*, *j*, *p*, *q*, and *y*. The lower zone is the erogenous zone, where you'll find the true measure of a writer's sexual and physical urges. Look at the lower loop of the *y* in Elvis's signature. It's large and inflated. Elvis wants his public to see him as a lean, mean, hip-swiveling sex machine.

That's the public Elvis. Now compare the large lower loop of the *y* in Elvis's signature to the lower loops in the body of his handwriting. Can you see how small and shrunken the lower loops are in Elvis's private script? Ex-wife Priscilla Beaulieu Presley, whom Elvis married in 1967, has said that after their honeymoon (when Priscilla became pregnant with Lisa Marie), they never made love again. They were married for six years.

When you see Elvis's big, snarlin', sexy signature beside his innocent-little-country-boy script, the contrast is rather startling.

Maybe it's these opposites in Elvis that make him so endearing and continue to fascinate us a generation after his tragic death at age forty-two.

The Choirboy and the Fox

Edward Hickman, a bright young honor student, volunteered at church and was the pride of his Sunday school. He was considered a model student and an asset to his community. That was until he kidnapped Marion Parker.

In December of 1927, 19-year-old Edward Hickman showed up at a Los Angeles public school to collect 12-year-old Marion Parker. He was able to convince Marion's teacher that the girl's father, a well-known banker, had been seriously injured in a car accident and that the girl had to go to the hospital immediately. Hickman disappeared with Marion, and over the next few days Mr. and Mrs. Parker received a series of cruel and taunting ransom notes demanding $1,500. The notes were signed "The Fox."

At the drop-off, Mr. Parker could see Marion in the passenger seat of Hickman's parked car. But as soon he handed Hickman the money, the car sped off. The police found Marion's legless body a short distance from the drop-off. Her eyes had been wired open to make her appear as if she were still alive. Police later found pieces of her body all over Los Angeles.

A week later, Hickman was picked up by two police officers in Oregon who recognized him from wanted posters. Back in Los Angles, Hickman told investigators: "This is going to get interesting before it's over. Marion and I were good friends, and we really had a good time when we were together and I really liked her. I'm sorry that she was killed." He never explained why he had killed and dismembered his friend (he said he needed the money to pay for bible college!), but by the time he was through talking, he had confessed to Marion's murder and a dozen armed robberies, including one in which he shot and killed a store clerk. Hickman was convicted of murder. He was executed by hanging at San Quentin in 1928.

Notice that Edward Hickman's signature looks fairly conventional. It leans to the right, meaning that, in public, he leans comfortably toward other people. The fact that his signature is large shows that Hickman acts extroverted and social. His signature is fairly consistent in size indicating he wants to appear consistent and reliable. The small, high, *i* dot shows that Hickman's a high achiever.

The body of Hickman's writing, however, tells a completely different tale. Do you see how his writing leans to the left? This is a sign that the real Edward Hickman is cold and reserved and pulls back emotionally. He will lean over backwards to cover up his true feelings.

His small printing indicates that, inside, Hickman feels shy and introverted.

Hickman's writing is erratic. Some of his words are written lightly while other words are written with a heavy pressure. This shows that Hickman cannot control his emotional responses and urges. He may be calm one minute and then suddenly, in a surge of sexual energy, he could pounce unpredictably.

And, look at those heavy *i* dots! Just wait until you find out what they mean in Chapter 12.

Illegible . . . But Not Unreadable

Even when signatures are indecipherable, they say a lot! These autographs may be unreadable, yet they still reveal key personality traits of the authors. An illegible signature means that the writer wants to keep his feelings hidden from the public and does not want his true self revealed. But sometimes, a closer look will reveal some very interesting things about a writer. Look at the clues below and guess who belongs to each of these mysterious signatures.

Look at the sharp angles in signature #1. You can almost see the tension and tightness in the author's hand. Angles appear in the signatures of workaholics who are sharp-minded, competitive, aggressive, determined, driven, and uptight.

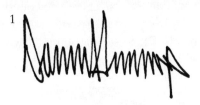

Writer #2 strings his illegible letters together with a long, squiggly thread. When threading makes a name illegible, it usually means that the writer is evasive and will try to wiggle out of situations.

Writer #3's name is the most difficult to decipher. Are those letters or Morse code? This is the signature of a very secretive and cryptic person who may have used Morse code in the military.

Signature #4 has both angles and threads. The angles show the hard-driven characteristics of writer #1; the threads show some of the sneakiness of writer #2. The combination of angles and threads can make for a brilliant politician.

Signature #5 begins with a sharp angle and spirals downward. The pressure is too heavy, a sign of an aggressive, forceful writer who imposes his will on others. There's no roundness or softness to this signature. And do you see the little slash in the cross-bar of the first letter (the *H*)? This x-formation indicates that the writer is preoccupied with death.

ANSWERS
1. Donald Trump
2. George W. Bush
3. Timothy McVeigh
4. Bill Clinton
5. Adolf Hitler

The Name Game

Get a pen and paper and list the names of four people you know: three people whom you like and admire and one who makes your hair stand on end and your blood boil.

Put your list aside. We'll take a look at what you wrote in a moment.

If you want to know what people really think of you, take a good look at your old birthday cards, Valentine's Day cards, and

Christmas cards. Did a certain someone write his name extra large and your name kind of teeny-weeny? Well, I hate to tell you this, but he thinks he's hot stuff and you're cold potatoes.

Dear Michelle, you are the greatest. love, John

On the other hand, if Sally from the garden club wrote your name large and bold and her name small and delicate, she sees you as a champion rose and herself as a shrinking violet.

Dear Louise Thank you for inviting me. Sincerely Sally

If your names are about equal in size, or the writer's name is just slightly larger than yours, then the writer considers you to be an equal.

Hi Lisa, Nice seeing you again. Your Friend,

*   *   *

Now, let's take a look at that list. Do you notice any difference between the names of the three people you admire and the name of the one who makes you squirm? If you look closely enough you'll probably see a difference.

Chances are you wrote the jerk's name smaller and lighter than the other names. This is because, subconsciously, you don't want to give this person as much energy or importance as the others.

If you wrote the jerk's name with heavier pressure than the names of the people you admire, it means that you are putting too much energy into the anger you feel towards him or her.

If you aligned the jerk's name far to the right of the names of your pals, it means that you want to push this person out of your life.

And you thought a name was just a name!

PART II

Stop Reading and Start Running!

⌒

5

Dirty Rotten Scoundrels

He loved to talk about everything. He told you about his favorite foods, his travels abroad, his Aunt Marge in Omaha, his second grade teacher, and his cat Fluffy. The only thing that he neglected to mention was his wife in Wichita, his other wife in Minneapolis, yet another wife in Laredo, and his recent engagement to a widow in Phoenix . . .

Your brother-in-law the stockbroker offers you a chance to double your investment in six months.
"Don't pass this up," he says. "An opportunity like this doesn't come along every day."
"Are you sure?" you ask.
"Trust me," he says.
You reach for your checkbook. He wouldn't lie to you, right? After all, he is your brother-in-law . . .

Liar, Liar

Look at the two handwriting samples on the next page. One of these writers is lying. Is it John or Tom?

Dear Michelle,
Sorry. I never showed up
at your party. I got   a   flat tire.

Love, John

Dear Michelle,
Sorry I missed your party, but I had
a little "accident." My cigarette
fell into my pants cuff and my
pants caught on fire! Yikes!
Hope to see you soon!

Tom

John is the liar. How can you tell? It takes more effort to lie than to tell the truth. A liar must think about what he is going to say. Do you see the gaps between the words "got," "a" and "flat" in John's note? That wide space is where John hesitated in his writing, while his brain conjured up a lie.

Anytime you see an abnormal gap between two words, there has been an interruption in the writer's thinking processes. Sometimes, an interruption is just that—an interruption. The writer got distracted in the middle of a sentence (the phone rang, the dog barked, etc.). However, an unusually wide space between two words is often a sign of that the writer is about to conjure up a real whopper.

Also notice how John writes the words "flat tire." The writing becomes much smaller and tighter.

Handwriting is a lot like body language. If a person speaks

softly as they falsely explain their whereabouts on the night in question, their writing will become smaller and lighter when they are lying. Or if they talk real loud and flail their arms when they tell a tale, then their writing will be larger and less controlled as they scribe their fib.

Signs of a Lyin', Cheatin', Cold Dead Beatin' Two-timin', Double-dealin', Mean Mistreatin' Scoundrel

The letters *a* and *o* are the communication letters. Think of these letters as little mouths. When a writer's *a*'s and *o*'s are open at the top, that writer likes to talk, and will find it difficult to keep a secret. When they are completely closed at the top, the writer is someone you can trust to take your secret to the grave. But when a writer's *a*'s and *o*'s are distorted or unclear, trust not.

Writers with *a*'s and *o*'s that are open at the bottom are bottom feeders who will eat you up and spit you out. They communicate in such a deceptive and distorted way, that nothing they say is believable. Jeffrey Dahmer's *o*'s and *a*'s were a sign of his voracious appetite for lying.

Slashes through *a*'s and *o*'s, known as "forked tongue strokes," are signs of a conniving, scheming liar. Notice the slash in O. J. Simpson's O.

O's or *a*'s that are filled with ink indicate that the writer communicates in dark, muddied ways. Jack the Ripper's muddied *o*'s in "bloody" convey the darkness of his message.

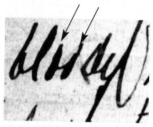

Of course, never look at just one *a* or *o*. It's possible that the writer's elbow just got bumped while she was writing and she might not be a dirty rotten scoundrel after all!

Spy Test

If you wanted to hire a spy who wouldn't spill the beans, would you hire Candidate A or B?

A

Dear Mr. Spymaster:

I am applying for the job that I saw advertised in the newspaper as a spy. I believe you will find that I am a perfect spy.

B

I am here to apply for the spy job.

The answer is A, the spy whose communications letters—and lips—are sealed.

The Wedding Planner

If your fiancé leaves out one or two itty-bitty details about his life (like the fact that he's already married), can your relationship still work?

Betty told me she was shocked when she discovered the truth about Harry, the man she had dated for two years:

> *I recently suffered a most rude awaking when I discovered that the gentle, sweet, handsome man I fell in love with, the man who asked me to marry him, had been lying to me. The biggest secret that he kept from me was his current marriage! I discovered that he had been lying to me by looking up the deed to his house.*
>
> *Upon being confronted, his excuse was that he didn't want to tell me until after his divorce was finalized, as he feared losing me. During our relationship, he frequently discussed marriage plans and our future together. He went as far as planning our wedding and putting the plans on paper.*
>
> *Can you tell me whether this man is safe to forgive and ever trust as a friend?*

Find Ring
Set Date January?
Clothing - Wedding Dress
Colors
Who will marry us?
Honeymoon.

Handsome Harry's flamboyant script and ornately embellished letters show me that he can be quite the actor, gifted at embellishing the truth.

You know that o's and a's that are tightly closed at the top mean that the writer is tight-lipped and secretive. Look at way Harry made his o in the word "Who." He not only closed his o at the top, he made sure it was sealed tight by finishing it at the bottom. There is no way this writer would leave even a slight gap at the top. He's so secretive that he won't even tell himself the truth.

Why would a married man make such a show of planning a wedding that couldn't be? Why would he care about the "Wedding Dress, colors, party, food, reception, cutlery, decorations, cake, champagne, music, entertainment . . ."? Given his ultra-flowery and feminine handwriting, I wonder if Handsome Harry's wedding fantasy is more about proving to Betty that he's the marrying kind—or proving to himself that, all things being equal, he'd rather be the bride.

Betty asked if it's safe for her to be friends with a man who pretended to plan the details of their wedding, but forgot to tell her that he has a wife.

There are many things in a friend we should desire . . . three of them being that he's not a fake, a phony, or a liar.

The Boss from Hell

Miriam had worked at the same dental office for ten years. She wrote to me about her new supervisor, who was making Miriam and her coworkers miserable:

Ever since Dr. Annie joined the group two years ago, it's been hell for all of us. Dr. Annie is the most evil woman I've ever met. She has written all the women in the office disparaging notes, belittling them and their work. I am enclosing the note she wrote to me. I realize that you don't know

me, but the letter she wrote—it's like she's talking about her-
self—not me.

Following is the text of the letter Miriam received from Dr.
Annie:

> *Your lack of care and commitment to your job and most*
> *aspects of your job is profoundly appalling. Your office*
> *manager skills are so poor. I am amazed at how incompetent,*
> *sloppy, and disorganized you continue to be. You have no*
> *leadership capabilities, rather you intimidate and bully any-*
> *body who doesn't go along with your personal, self-centered,*
> *power-hungry ways. You are a con and a fake—a pathetic*
> *excuse of a human being.*
>
> *Dr. Annie*

See that sharp point inside the *a* in the word "capabilities"?
That's a "stinger." When you find stingers inside the communication letters, *o* or *a*, you know that the writer communicates with
sharp, piercing words.

Stinger writers also tend to be extreme in their sexual
lifestyles—they either abstain from sex entirely, or they become
sexaholics.

Now, take a good look at the *n* in the word "manager." See

how the pointed top of the second hump of the *n* looks like it could take a bite out of you? This stroke is called a "shark's tooth." Shark's teeth appear in the writing of people who are emotionally hungry—not just a little hungry, but voracious. If you get in their way when they are in a feeding frenzy, beware, because you could be in for a merciless bloodletting.

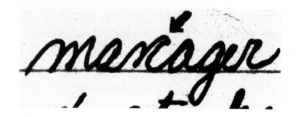

If you happen to see stingers or shark's teeth in the writing of your boss, it may be time to update your résumé.

Are You Dating a "Fake-out" Artist?

Charlie sat there in front of me with a handwriting sample of Kathy Sue. Charlie was looking for answers. How could he have been so wrong about his sweet Ms. Kathy?

"She seemed perfect," he said. "She was beautiful, athletic, and smart. I felt very lucky. After dating her for several months I introduced her to my family. Everybody liked her. I was planning on asking her to marry me.

"A few weeks ago, she told me that she wanted to visit her mother, who lives out of town. She said that she was short of cash, so I told her that her visit to her mother was my treat and I let her put her airplane ticket on my charge card. Well, it turns out that the airplane ticket wasn't the only thing that she put on my credit card. She wound up staying at a very expensive resort and spa at my expense. She told the people at the spa that I was going to join her. I didn't know about 'our' vacation, of course, so I didn't show up. I later found out that someone else did show up: her ex-boyfriend.

"She came up with all kinds of excuses. She even blamed the whole thing on me. Needless to say we are no longer together."

Dear honey,

you are wonderful

I'll be back in town

on 3/21/02

love,
Kathy

Look at the way Kathy Sue wrote the word "honey." Do you see that it could say something like "hiney" or "huny" or possibly even "Levej"? Now, look carefully at the way she combines the *e* and the *y* in "honey." Is that an *e* or a *y*? Both? Neither? Her ambiguous letter and word formations show that she knows how to disguise the truth. She's tricky and leaves the interpretation of events unclear so that she always has an out when she needs it.

Kathy Sue's numbers are also ambiguous. Notice the way she wrote the date. Is that 3/29/05? Or is it 6/21/02? When you meet someone who writes with ambiguous or trick numbers, you are almost always dealing with a bamboozler or an embezzler.

"Charlie," I told him, "don't feel too sorry that you missed your vacation. Look on the bright side. You lost your baggage without even leaving home. And in this case, that's a good thing!"

Family Business

The Kimes family business was a multinational enterprise with a broad range of practices and services, including arson, con games, forgery, fraud, grand theft, grifting, and the occasional murder.

They didn't need the money. They didn't have to work. Sante Kimes's husband (and Kenneth's father) was worth over $10 million. But this mother and son team had a drive to succeed on their own terms. They conned their way from Hawaii to New York, burning buildings, defrauding friends, enslaving housekeepers, robbing stores, forging documents, and murdering people.

In 1998, mother and son were arrested for the murder of Irene Silverman, a wealthy New York socialite. After Sante Kimes's trial for robbery, burglary, forgery, conspiracy, illegal possession of weapons, and murder, Justice Rena Uviller described her as "surely the most degenerate defendant who has ever appeared in this courtroom." Sante Kimes, who received a 120-year sentence, will spend the rest of her life in prison.

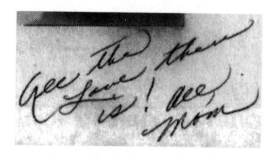

Take a close look at the first word. Can you make it out? In context, most people will be able to see the word "All." Now, cover all the other words with your fingers. Does it still look like "All"? Or does it look like "Ell" or "Gee" or maybe "Gel"?

Can you make out the word above "Mom"? Is that also "All" or "Ale"? It's quite different from the first "All." And what's that comma doing there, before the end of the word?

And what's that little dot to the right? Is it a period?

Not sure? Well, that's how a con artist works.

This sample of Sante Kimes's writing was on a photo she gave to her older son, Kent. She told Kent it was a photograph of her as a young woman. Years later, Kent realized that the subject in the photo was Elizabeth Taylor. Like so many others, he had been conned.

6

⌐

Sabotage in Their Script

Self-Sabotage

Johnny

Here's a letter I received from Johnny:

Dear Michelle,
   Hello. I'm a 32-year-old man who has spent the better part of 12 years in and out of prisons. I'm currently incarcerated. I thought it would be fun to write to you and get your opinion on my personality through my handwriting.
   Enclosed, if you will, is my favorite joke, "Got Grapes."
   Here it goes: So this duck walks into a bar, sits down, and says "Hey barkeep. Got any grapes?"
   The bartender says "No."
   The duck leaves. The next day the duck walks back into the bar, sits down and asks the bartender, "Hey barkeep, got any grapes?"
   Angered by the duck the bartender walks over to the duck and says, "Look pal, this is a bar. We serve drinks, not grapes! Next time you ask for grapes, I'm going to nail your bill to the bar."
   So the duck leaves. The next day the duck walks into the bar, sits down and asks.
   "Hey barkeep, got any nails?"

The bartender smiles and says, "No."
So the duck says, "Got any grapes?"
You are free to do what ever you like with this joke. I
look forward to hearing from you.
Yes, I am a very beautiful person!!
Johnny from Illinois
Note: I Love Me!

"Got any grapes?"

Yes I AM A VeRy !!
BeAutiful Person ..

NoTe.
I Love
Me.

What Johnny's got in his "Got?" Look carefully at the bottom of his *G*. Instead of curving upward, as we are taught in school, it curves downward. This backward claw formation, known as the "felon's claw," shows up in the handwriting of people who do things to sabotage themselves. Felon claw writers feel compelled to put themselves in self-destructive situations and do things that continually "mess up" their lives. In fact, over 80 percent of convicted felons have felon claws in their script. Of course, it doesn't mean that just because a writer makes a felon's claw, he's a felon. But where there are claws, there's cause for caution.

Think of a felon's claw as a cup that's been turned upside down. No matter how much love you give a felon claw writer, you cannot fill their cup. Though they crave love and attention, deep down they believe that nobody will ever really accept them. And if you're nice to them, eventually they'll turn on you and claw you in the back. Their bad behavior will make you reject them, which proves to them that they were right in the first place.

There's something else in Johnny's writing that reveals his true feelings about himself. Take a good look at his signature. Sure it's illegible, but one letter comes through loud and clear: *x*. Johnny's signature is one great big *x*. When a writer's signature or personal pronoun "I" turns into an *x* it shows that the writer feels as if his or her life has been ruined. These sad "x'ed-out" people worry and fantasize about death. Sometimes these gloomy thoughts are about other people's downfall and sometimes these morbid feelings are about the writer's own demise.

Richard Nixon

Crossing out your signature is like crossing out yourself. *X*'s in signatures are a sign of personal despair. Notice that between the election of 1968 and the Watergate crisis in 1974, Richard Nixon's signature changed into one big *x*.

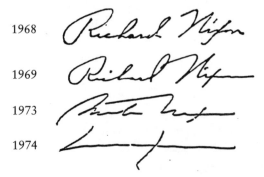

1968

1969

1973

1974

Napoleon Bonaparte

Look at how Napoleon Bonaparte's x'ed out his signature after his defeat at the Battle of the Nations at Leipzig.

John Allen Muhammad

Here's the signature of John Allen Muhammad who, with Lee Malvo, stalked and killed ten people in the Washington, DC area in October 2002. Notice the *X*-formations at the beginning and end of his signature (in the *J* and *d*).

Petitioner Signature

Jimi Hendrix

Jimi Hendrix's x'ed out signature reflects his self-destructive mantra: "I'm the one who's got to die when it's time for me to die, so let me live my life the way I want to." Two months before his twenty-eighth birthday, in a London hotel room Hendrix took too many pills and choked to death on his own vomit.

Jack Ruby

Did Dallas strip club owner Jack Ruby have a death wish? Notice how the man who shot Lee Harvey Oswald x'ed out the *J* in his first name. Ruby died of a pulmonary embolism in Parkland Hospital (the same hospital where JFK died) while awaiting trial.

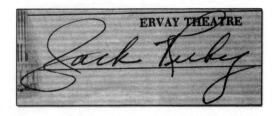

Corporate Sabotage

The felon's claw and crossed out signature are signs of writers who feel compelled to screw up their lives through various forms of self-sabotage. But what does it mean when someone you know crosses out *your* name?

Recently, I received a call from the CEO of a large Midwestern corporation. "Can you take a look at the handwriting of one of my employees?" he asked. The next morning, I received an envelope, but I was so bogged down with work at the time that I filed the envelope in my "get to later" pile. Later that day, the CEO called to see what I had learned about Shawn, his executive vice president. I explained my situation: "I have a murder case next week, and probably can't get to it before then." "I don't think you understand," he said. "This is urgent. Please, Michelle, I need your opinion as soon as possible."

"I'll call you tomorrow," I promised, as I shifted his unopened envelope into my "get to sooner than later" pile. That evening, as I studied Shawn's handwriting, I realized why the CEO was so concerned. Shawn's words looked innocent enough but there were red flags in his script that told me that the CEO was in a heap of trouble. The page was easy to read except for one name, which was written smaller, tighter, and more shriveled than the other words on the page. Through the middle of this hard-to-read name was a long slash, forming an X through the name. After looking at it for a few minutes, I realized that it was the name of the CEO.

Lower down on the page I noticed two other names: Shawn and Teddy. Shawn was written large, but the name "Teddy" was written even larger and bolder.

"I don't know how to put this to you," I told the CEO, "but Shawn doesn't like you very much. In fact, he will do anything to destroy you, and he's planning on doing it with someone named Teddy."

"Teddy, my computer guy? He's a heck of a nice guy. One of the nicest," replied the CEO. I asked him to fax me a sample of Teddy's handwriting. Teddy's writing had all the signs of a dirty rotten scoundrel, including forked tongue strokes and ambiguous numbers.

"I wouldn't trust your computer guy," I told the CEO. "He wants to take something from you. It could be money, equipment, or even information." The CEO replied, "If Teddy's a thief, he's the best actor I've ever seen."

A few days later, both Shawn and Teddy resigned. Teddy had already stolen one of the company's most valuable assets: computer files that contained detailed information about every one of the company's clients and contracts. As it turned out, Shawn and Teddy had been in cahoots for over a year. Their goal was to undermine the corporation, steal its top clients, and form their own business.

There are people who can smile in your face while they plot your demise. Sometimes the only clue to their knife-twisting schemes is the sabotage in their script.

7

Cruel and Unusual Letters

Here's an unusual signature:

I know you can't "read" it, but I'll bet you can read the message behind the signature. Before reading the next paragraph, write down what you see, including any images, symbols, or secret messages. Feel free to turn the book upside down. Hold it at different angles. Read it from left to right and from right to left. What is hidden in plain view?

The Arsenal in His Mind

On November 1, 2001, seven weeks after the attack on the World Trade Center, Qatar-based al-Jazeera television received a letter from Osama bin Laden, written in Arabic, calling on Muslims to fight a jihad or holy war against "the American Crusade." The letter was signed:

I can't read Arabic, but I have found that no matter what language or alphabet a writer may use, certain principles are universal. In any language, pen strokes that resemble knives, daggers, harpoons, or other weapons indicate dangerous and hostile thoughts. And when weapon-shaped letters or images are embedded in a writer's signature or personal pronoun "I," watch out.

Did you notice any weapon-shaped images in bin Laden's signature? Here are some of the weapons that I found:

Moving from right to left (the way Arabic is written):

Assault rifle:

Grenade with the pin pulled, ready to explode:

Bomb with a fuse:

Dead body with blood oozing from the head:

Scary stuff. But is the scariness intentional? Did bin Laden mean to put these symbols of war in his signature? Or were they so deeply planted in his brain that he couldn't help but express them in his signature? My bet is the latter. And in my mind, that makes this scary inkblot even scarier.

The Hawk

Sometimes I look at handwriting and see an image or a symbol in the writing that's so odd, it just begs for analysis.

A few years ago, I was called in to analyze a note written on the body of an older woman who had been brutally murdered. I noticed some strange doodles in the handwriting, little squiggles attached to many of the letters. The more I looked at the doodles, the more they reminded me of little footballs. I told the detectives that football played an important role in the writer's life. It turned out that the prime suspect had been a standout player on his college football team.

I always keep my eyes open for unusual shapes and symbols in handwriting. For instance, at a party, I met a handsome and debonair man. After the usual small talk, he asked me for my phone number. I responded by asking for his handwriting—a question most guys find a bit peculiar! He scrawled his name on a note pad. I noticed a weird scribble in the middle of his signature. It looked like a cartoon figure of some kind, with a profile that resembled the head and beak of a falcon or an eagle.

"Are you into cartoons?" I asked.

"No, not really. Why?" he said.

"Ummm . . . do you like birds?"

"Birds?"

"Falcons, eagles . . . hawks?"

His eyes lit up. "I love hawks," he replied. "In fact, in college my friends called me 'the Hawk.' 'Cause when I want something, I swoop down and grab it! How'd you know that I liked hawks?" he asked.

I pointed to the little scribble in his signature. He was totally unaware that he had drawn a cartoon of a hawk smack dab in the middle of his name.

We talked a bit more. He told me about his big old house in the country, with three stuffed hawks on the mantle and trophies from his hunting expeditions on the walls. "You'd love my house," he said. "It does get lonely at times, out in the middle of nowhere. I've got my five Doberman pinschers to keep me company, but sometimes, I could use some company of the human kind."

"I have a dog, too. Her name is Mageeloo," I said.

"Well, why don't you come up next weekend? You can bring your dog."

I pictured little Mageeloo (who weighs just seven pounds) and me in a big, dark, scary house with the Hawk and his five Dobermans. "Um, next weekend, I think I'll be away," I said. *And every weekend from now until the end of time,* I thought. I sure wasn't going to let hawk man swoop me off my feet!

Symbolic Gestures

Like the Hawk, most people are unaware of the messages that they subconsciously place in their script. Yet there are some people who consciously and deliberately put symbolism in their handwriting to represent something about themselves.

Remember Liberace's signature? Musicians often include the tools of their trade in their signatures.

Here's the signature of a drum major at a large Midwestern university.

And notice how Laci Peterson drew a little smiley face next to her name. Her friends and family remember the bright smile that lit up Laci's face, the smile that was such a big part of Laci's personality. That smile was Laci's trademark.

However, just because a writer puts on a happy face doesn't mean he's the happy-go-lucky type.

The Happy Face Killer

Laverne Pavlinac, a 57-year-old grandmother in Portland, Oregon, picked up the phone and called the police. "I know who raped and killed Taunja Bennett," she said.

Laverne claimed that she was forced to aid her 43-year-old boyfriend, John Sosnovske, in disposing of the body of his petite victim. In intricate detail, she told detectives how Sosnovske had placed a rope around Taunja's neck and raped her. She pointed out to the detectives where the body had been dumped. However, she could not answer any questions about where Taunja's purse or other personal belongings were.

Sosnovske denied any involvement in the crime, but with Pavlinac's detailed confession, the District Attorney easily won a guilty verdict. In 1991, John Sosnovske was sentenced to life imprisonment. Laverne Pavlinac received ten years.

Then Pavlinac recanted her confession. She claimed that she had read details of the murder in the newspaper. She said that she had made up the whole story about her boyfriend to teach him a lesson and end their stormy and abusive relationship. But, now, nobody was listening. Well, almost nobody.

During the trial, a message was found scrawled on a wall in a truck stop restroom: "Killed Tanya [sic] Bennett in Portland. Two people got the blame so I can kill again (Cut buttons off jeans— proof)" The message was signed with a happy face.

Soon, newspaper editors began receiving "Happy Face" letters. All were written in the same handwriting as the script on the restroom wall. The writer said he was a trucker and that he had murdered six women, including Taunja Bennett. Each letter had a happy face on top of the page. Police paid little attention to the letters, dismissing the writer as "just another crazy."

It was not until 1995 that investigators started to put the pieces together, including the handwriting evidence. After killing his girlfriend, a Canadian long-haul trucker named Keith Hunter Jesperson wrote a letter to his brother admitting that he was a serial killer. The handwriting on the letter matched the handwriting of the "Happy Face" killer.

After serving four years for a murder they did not commit, John Sosnovske and Laverne Pavlinac were released from prison. Keith Hunter Jesperson was convicted of murdering three women in Oregon and Washington and is serving the first of three consecutive life sentences in Oregon.

Were there red flags in Jesperson's handwriting that might have led police to take his letters more seriously?

To find the real Jesperson, we need to study his subconscious handwriting. For Jesperson, the happy face was a conscious disguise. It was his calling card, his ruse, the trademark of his twisted killing game. Writing or doodles that are consciously crafted or stylized can mask a writer's true motives and personality. But writing that streams from the subconscious reveals the person behind the mask.

This sample is from a note Jesperson wrote from jail.

There's a symbol embedded in Jesperson's signature that reveals a lot about the man. Look at the word "Hunter." Do you notice something unusual where the *t* and *e* intersect? No, that's not a chicken's foot (in the signature of a chicken farmer, maybe, but not this one). It's a pitchfork, also known as a devil's fork. This fiendish formation appears subconsciously in the handwriting of writers who feel bedeviled with satanic obsessions and fantasies.

See anything else of a satanic nature? Well, of course, there's Jesperson's drawing of a she-devil. She's got quite a prominent tail! Compare that tail to the tail of the *n* in "Jesperson." Now, do you have any doubt about that devil's fork planted in Jesperson's middle name?

For years, Jesperson fooled those around him into thinking he was a nice, fun-loving guy. But his handwriting shows that behind his nice-guy facade, his impish doodles, and his trademark happy face, is the stone cold heart of a serial killer.

The Cruel and Brutal Club

Red stains on the carpet,
Red stains on your knife
Oh Dr. Buck Ruxton you murdered your wife.
The nursemaid saw you,

And threatened to tell,
Oh Dr. Ruxton, you killed her as well.
—British schoolyard ditty

Dr. Buck Ruxton was a popular and well-respected physician in Lancaster, England. Unfortunately, he also had a raging temper. A jealous and controlling man, he publicly accused his wife, Isabella, of having an affair.

On September 14, 1935, Isabella Ruxton and her maid, Mary Rogerson, went missing. Parts of their mutilated bodies were later found wrapped in newspaper in a ravine under a bridge in Scotland. The body parts were so jumbled that the case was nicknamed the Jigsaw Murders. The victims' fingertips had been chopped off to prevent fingerprint identification.

The murderer did leave some clues, however. For example, the newspaper used to wrap the bodies was a special edition of the *Sunday Graphic* sold only in Lancaster. And forensic science provided new methods to identify the victims: Investigators superimposed an X-ray of one of the skulls found in the ravine onto a life-size photo of Isabella's head. It was a perfect match. Entomologists established the time of death by studying the maggots crawling on the bodies.

The evidence pointed to Dr. Buck Ruxton. At his trial, Ruxton lost his temper and shouted, "Do I look like a murderer? It is not my nature. My blood is boiling now."

Ruxton was found guilty and sentenced to death. Before his execution he wrote this confession note.

Look at the thickness of ink at the bottom of the letter *y* in the word "Mary" and the *p* in the word "present." A writer must apply considerable force to the pen to accumulate this thick glob of ink at the bottom of a letter. These club-shaped lower stems show a writer who is likely to strike first and ask questions later.

Here is another club-stroke writer who used brute force to get his way.

This is the writing of Adolf Hitler from 1943. Look at the heavy, thick blob of ink at the bottom of the down stroke in his insignia. Picture the movement of Hitler's hand as he made this stroke as his fist smashing down onto a podium.

The Strangler Stroke

Here is an image of a hangman's noose created by a serial killer who "put down" his victims using a simple cord or rope. Now, if one of your coworkers repeatedly left drawings of a hangman's noose on your desk, you might become concerned. But no one seemed to notice anything strange about the man who created this image and used it again and again to sign his name.

The noose is actually the first letter in the signature of Dennis Rader, the Kansas animal control officer who bound, tortured, and killed at least ten people between 1974 and 1991. And not only were his coworkers, family members, neighbors, and fellow church members unaware of its significance—Dennis Rader himself probably had no clue that every day, subconsciously, every time he signed his name, he was providing a clue into his secret life.

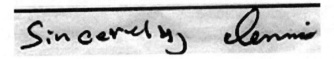

Compare the obvious, conscious symbolism in the BTK killer's self-designed "logo" (below) with the more subtle, subconscious symbolism in his signature.

Letter formations that resemble a strangler's rope or noose are called "strangler strokes." Let's look at three other convicted killers with strangler strokes in their script.

Cookie Monster Want Do Bad Things

Harrison "Marty" Graham had some strange habits, but those who knew him considered him amusing and harmless. He liked to walk around with a Cookie Monster puppet, entertaining his buddies by talking "Cookie Monster" talk. His neighbors in North Philadelphia, however, weren't so keen on Graham. They complained about the awful odor coming from his apartment.

On a scorching hot summer day in 1987, knowing his landlord was about to evict him from the apartment, Graham nailed his bedroom door shut and vacated his apartment. When the police broke down the door, they found the decaying bodies of seven women. A week later, Harrison Graham walked into a police station and turned himself in. He claimed that he didn't kill anyone. He was innocent. The bodies had been there when he moved in and he was just too afraid to tell anyone. Eventually, Graham admitted that he had raped and strangled all seven women. Those strangler strokes in Graham's handwriting are no coincidence.

See those large, unnecessary loops in the *n* in "Situation" and the *G* in "Graham"? Those are strangler strokes.

The Boston Strangler

Between June 14, 1962 and January 4, 1964, eleven women in the Boston area were strangled to death in their own apartments. When handyman Alberto DeSalvo was arrested in November 1964 for sexually assaulting a young newlywed in her apartment, he told police "If you knew the whole story, you wouldn't believe it." Over the next few months, DeSalvo told investigators his story. He said had committed nearly two thousand break-ins and sexual assaults in Massachusetts, Rhode Island, Connecticut, and New Hampshire. A few months later, he confessed to being the Boston Strangler.

Notice the noose-like strangler stroke in this sample taken from DeSalvo's confession:

In 1967 DeSalvo was tried and convicted for armed robbery, assault, and battery. One witness testified that DeSalvo
had held a knife to her throat and sexually assaulted her after
gagging her with her panties and tying her to the bed with her
other clothing.

Never charged with the Strangler murders, DeSalvo was held
in a state mental hospital for three years. In 1967, he was transferred to a maximum security prison, where he was stabbed to
death by another inmate in 1973. You'll learn more about
DeSalvo and his obsessions in Chapter 11.

Scott Peterson

Scott Peterson had reported his wife Laci missing on Christmas
Eve, 2002. But in the months that followed, Peterson's actions
made it clear that he didn't expect her to return. Two weeks
after Christmas, Scott bought himself a present. He ordered the
Playboy Channel installed in their home. Five days later, he had
upgraded to a hard-core pornography channel.

By the end of January, Scott met with a real estate agent to
explore selling their house, and soon after, he sold Laci's car.

On April 18, 2003, four days after the decomposed bodies of
his wife and baby washed up on a beach in Northern California,
police officers in Southern California stopped Scott Peterson driving his red Mercedes toward the Mexican border. With a goatee
and his hair dyed blonde, Peterson was nearly unrecognizable. As
he was handcuffed, Peterson asked the officer, "Have they found
my wife and son?"

Scott Peterson was charged with the intentional, deliberate,
premeditated murder of his 27-year-old pregnant wife Laci Peterson and their unborn child.

Though Scott Peterson was convicted on overwhelming cir-
cumstantial evidence, investigators never identified a murder
weapon. Sample A is Peterson's signature on his booking form.
Do you see the large loop on the right side of Peterson's signature?

A

B

C

The handwriting of murderers often contains their weapons of choice. The writing of DeSalvo (B) and Graham (C) contains unmistakable strangler strokes. Does the strangler stroke in Peterson's signature provide a clue as to how his wife died?

What should you do if meet someone with weapon strokes, club strokes, or strangler strokes in his handwriting? RUN LIKE MAAAADDDDDDDDDDDDD!

8

Crackups and Meltdowns

What do these three people have in common?

1. A boy who washes his hands over and over until his skin is red and raw
2. A woman who plucks a few hairs from her left eyebrow to make it symmetrical with her right eyebrow and ends up plucking out each and every hair on her face
3. Milton, a writer with overly connected writing, lots of extra squiggles, and reversed letters in his handwriting

Last year, I received this letter from Milton:

Dear Michelle.

All of my life I have had a propensity towards extreme behavior. While never harmful to myself or another person, I tend to get my mind focused upon something and this becomes a personal obsession for me. For example, I started purchasing bars of soap a few years back. At first it was just one of those things, then I began to realize one day that I had over 5,000 bars of soap in my garage. I do this with other things. I only date women with blond hair. I only eat one kind of Chinese food—chicken egg foo young. Whatever it is—a favorite music group, work of art, intellectual con-

cept—I get a focus on and develop a passion for it. Anything else that fails to hold my interest—I ignore. Am I crazy?
Sincerely, Milton in Missouri

The clues that Milton has Obsessive Compulsive Disorder (OCD) are not only in his behaviors, as he described them, but in his handwriting.

For example, look at the doodad on the beginning stroke of his *W* in the words "While" and "Whatever" below.

Notice that the letters *g* and *s* in the word "things" are more than a little bizarre. And look very closely at the word "then."

Can you see that the *n* is haphazardly attached to the end of the word? His personal pronoun "I" is reversed and goes in the wrong direction. Also, look at the unnecessary thingamajigs in the word "realize." The letter *a* has an extra stroke above it and the *l* in "realize" has an added loop.

began to realize

Throughout his handwriting there are unnecessary strokes—all those doodads and thingamajigs—that don't belong. Like the five thousand bars of soap in his garage, they're signs of obsessive-compulsive behavior.

Enough Already!!!!!

Extra thingamajigs aren't the only superfluous doodads that show obsession. Anything that's overly done shows that a writer has trouble knowing when enough is enough!!! We've all seen people who like to underline and underline . . . or. . . . use, excessive, punctuation!!!!!

Sidney mailed me a letter. Before I even opened his letter I could tell a lot about him. There was something strange about the way he addressed the envelope. He wrote "Michelle Dresbold or Handwriting Doctor." He underlined practically every word and double underlined the word "or." What does it mean when someone underlines words? Well, that depends.

Michelle Dresbold or Handwriting Doctor
c/o, Oasis Newsfeatures
PO Bx 2023

It's one thing to write: "Do not bend. <u>Breakable</u>," in the hope that your package will arrive in one piece. But when a writer underlines words randomly, it indicates an inability to determine what is important and what is not.

Now let's open up Sidney's letter.

Not only has Sidney continued to underline words randomly, he's added unnecessary quotation marks, exclamation marks, and asterisks throughout the letter.

Three things it's best to avoid: petting a strange dog named Killer, gambling with a guy named Lucky, and hiring someone who underlines every other word to make your business decisions!

All Mixed Up

Where there's erratic writing, an erratic writer can't be far away. Erratic writers often mix capitals and lower case letters or write teeny-weeny letters next to great big letters. One moment, their writing leans one way, and the next it leans the other way. An unpredictable script shows an unpredictable mind.

Mr. Unpredictable

After Barbara got divorced she sent me this letter:

> *I'm sending you a copy of my ex-husband's signature, as I've always found it quite odd.*
>
> *John is a cruel, abusive, paranoid and controlling man one minute . . . and the nicest guy in the world the next. He is sneaky and lies as easily as he breathes. He steals from his employer and feels justified doing so.*
>
> *What did I miss? The abuse did not start until after we were married.*

To keep my brother Joel-the-attorney happy, I can only show you a "simulated" version of John's signature below. However, if John's real name was John M. Smith, it would look almost exactly like this:

Notice how Mr. Smith's first name slants sharply to the left. His middle initial is straight up and down. And his last name slants far to the right.

Left-slanted writers are emotionally repressed and withdrawn. No matter how hard you push or pull, you won't know what's going on in their heads. Backhanded writers, like Timothy McVeigh (Zsa Zsa's opposite in Chapter 1) will lean over backwards to avoid letting you know anything about them.

Vertical writers need to be in control of their emotions. Like James Bond, they strive to be cool, calm, and collected at all times. "Head over heart" is their motto.

Extreme right-slanted writers often let their emotions get the best of them. When they lose control, they can be jealous, romantic, impulsive and volatile.

The instability of Mr. Smith's signature—as indicated by the wildly different slants—shows that, emotionally, he's one very unpredictable and unstable man.

The moral of this story: Don't make connections . . . with a gal or guy whose handwriting slants in all directions!

Prisoner #74539478

Here's the writing of Prisoner # 74539478, a twenty-something felon who is seeking a "sugar daddy" to take care of him after his release from prison.

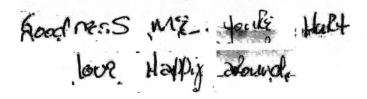

Notice how the size of his letters jumps around from big to small. For instance, in the word "you're," there's an itsy-bitsy *y*, teeny-weeny *o* and *u*, a great big *R*, and a medium *E*. This writer's moods can fluctuate more than the Dow Jones average. In the morning he could be good old Charlie Brown, but by the afternoon, watch out, because he could be bad, bad Leroy Brown.

If You've Always Wished You Had Perfect Handwriting, Read This!

Overly slow and carefully constructed writing is called "persona writing." Persona writers feel that if they don't take the time to make things look "just right," someone might discover their faults.

> I NEED HELP LEARNING ABOUT MYSELF. I WAS A VERY SHY
> PERSON GROWING UP. I DIDN'T FIND IT EASY TO MAKE NEW
> FRIENDS; THEREFORE, I WANTED TO BE MORE OUTGOING AND

This young man's perfect and machine-like writing shows that he doesn't want to say, feel, or do anything that may not appear perfect. He's afraid that someone (including himself) will see that he's, well, human:

Hi! I am a seventeen-year-old boy from Quincy, Illinois. I am writing to you because I need help learning about myself. I was a very shy person growing up. I didn't find it easy to make new friends; therefore I wanted to be more outgoing and bold. With a lot of effort, I was somewhat able to make that transition. I made an effort to open up more, but it seems that I still find it hard to show my true feelings. For example, I am not able to cry and let out my feelings when I feel hurt or sad, I cannot vent my anger properly (it builds until it suddenly explodes), and sometimes I get confused about what I am feeling. I have almost lost someone that I really care about because of my inability to put words to how I feel. Sometimes, I find myself saying one thing while meaning something else.

The Shooter

Look at these two handwriting samples. Who is more likely to "crack up," writer #1 or writer #2?

Writer 1

Writer 2

I sure hope you said writer #2, because writer #1 is me! When you see handwriting that is too mechanical, with that "typewriter look," the writer is overcompensating for fear of losing control. And when these "too perfect" writers do lose control, they often go completely berserk!

Writer #2 is Ronald Taylor. I've never met Ronald Taylor, but I almost became one of his victims.

On March 1, 2000, I was hungry and running late. I decided to do something that I rarely do: grab a quick bite at a fast-food joint. (Normally, I'm a tofu-and-broccoli person.) As I approached the restaurant at about 11:30 AM, a police officer stopped and redirected me.

"Roads blocked, turn around."

"Great," I thought, "now, not only am I late for my meeting, I'm starving!"

Luckily I was running about fifteen minutes late, because at around 11:15 AM, Ronald Taylor had entered the McDonald's restaurant where I had planned to grab a Big Mac. Within minutes, he had shot and killed three people and wounded two others.

A few months after the incident, the Allegheny County DA asked me to compare Taylor's known writing—including letters, a "hit list," and a notebook filled with football scores, doodles, and racial epithets—to anonymous hate mail received by several people before the shootings. I concluded that Taylor had written all of the anonymous letters.

The jury convicted Ronald Taylor on forty-six criminal charges, including three counts of first-degree murder. Taylor was sentenced to death.

Criminal Intent

When the CEO of an ice cream company received a handwritten letter that said: "Guess which batch has the poison," I was called in to investigate. I asked a group of employees to write phrases that included the letters in the note. As the employees wrote, I observed them. One man sat far in the back of the room and wrote painfully slowly. Before I even looked at his script, I guessed that he was the writer of the threatening note. After looking at the scripts of all the employees, I identified "Mr. Slow-poke" as the anonymous writer. Eventually, he confessed. On those occasions where I interview a group of suspects, I've noticed that the writer who sits the farthest away from me and writes the slowest is almost always the culprit.

If you were to interview convicted felons and ask them simple questions like "What did you have for lunch today?" you would notice that many of them will pause, ponder, and then speak very slowly. Why? Because they are so used to covering up that it is difficult for them to answer freely and spontaneously.

Please read the following paragraph. I know it looks a bit bizarre but I guarantee that you can read it:

I cdnuolt blveiee taht I cluod acultaly uesdnatnrd waht I was rdanieg. The phaonmneal pweor of the hmuan mnid. It deosn't mttaer in waht odrer the ltteers in a wrod are, the olny iprmoatnt tnhig is taht the frist and lsat ltteer be in the rghit pclae. The rset can be a taotl mses and you can sltil raed it wuothit a porbelm. Tihs is bcuseae the huamn mnid deos not raed ervey lteter by istlef, but the wrod as a wlohe. Amzanig huh!

When you read, your brain picks out what's important and fills in the rest. Similarly, when you write or speak naturally and spontaneously, you don't need to stop and think about every letter individually. Writing should be free and spontaneous. The most natural and efficient writing flows from the brain to the hand effortlessly.

Master of Disguise

Slow, monotonous writing can cover up the most evil of intentions. Writers who use persona writing to hide their true personalities can be like wolves in sheep's clothing.

When Kenneth Bianchi wrote this letter, the tall, dark, and handsome Bianchi had just become a new father to a baby boy. His long-term girlfriend, Kelli Boyd, described him as kind and gentle, the type of person who couldn't hurt anyone. His boss respected him and considered him to be a dedicated and responsible employee.

Let's look at Bianchi's handwriting.

Bianchi's script has that labored, mechanical look that results when a writer is trying to make his handwriting look perfect. The baseline (the invisible line that we write on when we use an unlined piece of paper) is straight—so straight that it looks as if he used a ruler under each line. Maybe he did and maybe he didn't! It really doesn't matter. When someone uses a ruler to write, it shows a deep-seated fear of losing control. And if a writer takes the extraordinary amount of time necessary to write as if he used a ruler, he's afraid that if he relaxes even an inch he will go mad.

Unknown to his girlfriend, friends, and coworkers, this kind, gentle, dedicated, and responsible man was also the predator known as the Hillside Strangler. Kenneth Bianchi terrorized the city of Los Angeles for five months between 1977 and 1978. He was involved in the rapes and murders of at least ten women. He dumped their bodies on hillsides near the freeway.

After his arrest (and after he watched a TV movie called *Sybil*), Bianchi claimed that he suffered from multiple personality disorder. Four psychiatrists backed up his claims, describing how Bianchi's lost memories and hidden identities had revealed themselves under hypnosis. But Bianchi's Sybil defense was just another facade. Judge Ronald George was stunned that so many psychiatrists could have "naively swallowed Mr. Bianchi's story, hook, line and sinker, almost confounding the criminal justice system."

⟵

9

The Dictator,
the Mobster, and Me

In the hand of a verbal abuser, a pen can be a blunt instrument or a razor-sharp scalpel. Their attack-dog approach to communication is not limited to paper, however. In the course of a normal conversation, these verbal athletes can cut you down to size or clobber you into submission.

Pointed Arguments

Roxanne has been married for less than a year, and already her marriage is on the rocks.

My husband is a doctor and well respected in the community. When other people are around he is personable, kind, and protective of me. My family and friends love him and tell me that I'm so lucky to have gotten such a good catch. However, when we get home it is another story. He belittles me, terribly. I have always been considered pretty but he tells me that my hair is ugly and that I'm not as pretty as I used to be. He tells me that everything I do is wrong. For example, yesterday I went grocery shopping and put the food away in the refrigerator. He screamed at me because I put the broccoli on the wrong shelf. When there is a problem, he refuses to discuss it and throws objects into the wall. Our walls are ridden with holes. He falls asleep every night in front of the television and waits until the middle of the night to go to bed. I find myself sleeping on the edge of the bed praying that he won't touch me. To make matters worse, my husband is a psychiatrist! I feel as if there is no one I can talk to and I'm in this jail for life. Please help . . .

Let's look at the good (or not so good) doctor's handwriting.

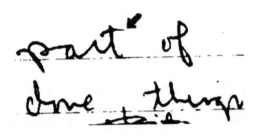

Look very carefully at the horizontal crossbar on his letter *t*. Do you notice that it thins out to a sharp, stabbing point? People with these *t* bars have piercing tongues. They are critical—the worst kind of critical. When you least expect it, they cut you down with their sharp words.

The Control Freak

And if the writer's *t* bars end with sharp stabbing points and thrust downward you're dealing with an individual who will not only cut you down but will cut you down and spit you out.

As Martha says, she's been living with a control freak for years and it's driving her mad:

My husband is a very controlling person. He is always leaving me "to do" notes. I am enclosing a recent "to do" note that he left for me to do this weekend.

If I don't do what he says he goes into a tirade. When I tell him I have my own things to do, he tells me that I'm lazy. If

I forget something he's told me he tells me that I should get checked for Alzheimer's. When I express my opinion he tells me I'm wrong and "everybody" knows that I'm wrong. When I say, "Who's everybody?" he just replies, "Everybody who knows anything."

Here are five signs that you're married to a control freak:

1. He swears that he wouldn't tell you how to breathe correctly if you weren't "doing it all wrong."
2. When he asks, "Honey, how are you doing?" he doesn't wait for your reply. He answers for you.
3. When you go to a restaurant, he not only insists on ordering for you, he insists on sending your meal back to the chef.
4. He installs an employee time clock in the bedroom.
5. He insists on receiving an itemized inventory not only of your daily food input, but of your "output" as well.

Another sure-fire sign that you're married to a control freak is that his *t* bars slant downhill. Think of these downward *t* bars as the writer's fist slamming down on the table. As the hand crashes down, the writer demands that things be done his way or no way.

Look at the word "practice" in this to-do list Martha's husband wrote for her. Notice how his *t* bars travel downward. Also, look at how his *t* bars end with sharp points.

The Good Neighbor

George let his old neighbor Jack, Jack's wife Lou Anne, and Jack's four kids (all under the age of six) stay with him for four weeks. When George found out that Jack wanted to move his family into a home without any electricity, water, or plumbing, he expressed his concerns to Lou Anne. Shortly afterwards "the gang" moved out. Recently, George received the following letter. Now George has another concern: "Is this man dangerous?"

> *The hospitality you and your family extended to my family allowing us to have a temporary home for people and animals is greatly appreciated and we are thankful.*
>
> *Your verbal attack upon my wife on Monday night brings to the forefront some issues that need to be clarified between you and me.*
>
> *I do not believe that extending hospitality to someone gives you the right to evaluate, judge and condemn their beliefs, children, life choices, or where they choose to defecate.*
>
> *As a husband and father I will do what is necessary to protect my family. In closing, I would like to offer you one piece of advice: DON'T YOU EVER VERBALLY ATTACK OR ABUSE MY WIFE AGAIN!*

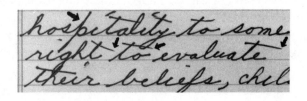

Is Jack dangerous? Although it's unlikely he's a serial killer, I wouldn't want to get into an argument with him—and I sure wouldn't want to visit his place without my Port-a-Potty and a case of Wet Naps!

Like the downward *t* bars of Martha's husband, many of Jack's *t* bars also slant downward, showing that he's one of those dogmatic types who are only too happy to let you know it's his way or the highway.

Oh, but we have more than Jack's tough *t*'s—we also have his pugilistic *p*'s.

When the initial stroke of a lower case *p* spikes far above the middle zone, you're looking at a pugilistic *p*. The pugilistic *p* shows up in the writing of people who are extremely argumentative. The higher the initial stroke rises above the middle zone, the more tenaciously pugnacious the writer.

If you say the sky is blue, they'll say it's green, and they'll never back down—no matter how many color wheels or meteorologists you put in front of their face.

Pugilistic *p*'s are common in the handwriting of trial attorneys, who go into court armed for combat with their swift words.

If you meet people who have tough *t*'s and pugilistic *p*'s, my advice is to give them no advice. They're not going to listen anyway.

The Dictator

Before he started smoking those big cigars, Fidel Castro, age fourteen, wrote a letter to Franklin Delano Roosevelt, president of the United States:

6-November-1940

President of the United States.

If you like, give me a ten dollars bill green american, in the letter, because never, I have not seen a ten dollars bill green american and I would like to have one of them, My address is:

Sr. Fidel Castro, Colegio de Dolores, Santiago de Cuba. Oriente. Cuba.

I don't know very English but I know very much Spanish and I suppose you don't know very Spanish but you know very English because you are American but I am not American.

(Thank you very much.) Good by, Your friend,

F Castro

Fidel Castro

If you want iron to make your ships I will show to you the bigest (minas) of iron of the land. They are in Mayari. Oriente Cuba.

If Roosevelt had sent the young wheeler-dealer that ten dollars American, Castro might have gone into the ship-building business rather than politics.

One thing is clear from his handwriting—even at the age of fourteen, Fidel Castro was no pushover. With those tall extensions on the initial strokes of his *p*'s in the words "Spanish" and "suppose," he could have been the captain of the debate team. It's not surprising Castro was a lawyer before he went into politics.

Castro is famously argumentative. His fiery speeches, which often go on for hours, are filled with facts and figures to support his arguments. (Castro once held the record for delivering the world's longest speech.)

The Mobster

Pugilistic writers have an intense need to be right and to win. And when challenged or pushed too far, they stop arguing and start whacking. One such writer was Alphonse Capone. Notice the tall, spiky *p*'s in Capone's signature when he was nineteen, taken from his draft registration card.

Born in Brooklyn, New York in 1899, Capone began his life of crime at a young age. After dropping out of school in the sixth grade, Capone worked his way up in the "growth industries" of bootlegging, racketeering, prostitution, and gambling.

By the time he was thirty years old, Capone's empire was worth over $62 million. The crime boss wasn't shy about how he obtained his wealth. "I make my money by supplying a public demand. If I break the law, my customers, who number in the hundreds of the best people in Chicago, are as guilty as I am. The only difference is that I sell and they buy. Everybody calls me a racketeer. I call myself a businessman." Of course, one difference between Capone and most other businessmen was that when he wanted to expand his business, he simply knocked off his competitors.

In 1931, two years after the famous St. Valentine's Day massacre, the Feds finally nailed Capone for tax evasion. Sent to Atlanta, the toughest of Federal prisons, Alphonse Capone was able to persuade the warden to give him special privileges. He convinced the guards to work for him and procured expensive furniture for his cell along with a typewriter, rugs, mirrors, a set of Encyclopaedia Britannica, and a radio.

But soon word spread of Capone's privileged life behind bars, leading the government to transfer him to Alcatraz. Finally "Scarface" had met his match. "It looks like Alcatraz has got me licked."

Here is Capone's signature from the late 1930s:

Scientists have found that abnormalities in handwriting can be indicators of disease. Take a second look at Al Capone's later signature. Do you notice anything unusual? There's something growing inside the *A* in "Al." It's very possible that this abnormality in Capone's writing was related to the disease that was ravaging his system. During his four and a half years at Alcatraz, Capone began showing the symptoms of dementia, a result of syphilis. He had apparently become infected with the disease in his early days as a brothel owner.

After his release from Alcatraz, Capone quietly deteriorated at his lush mansion on Palm Island near Miami. In 1947, the pugnacious mobster was finally beaten by an adversary he couldn't argue with, an enemy he couldn't whack. At the age of forty-eight, Capone died from complications of syphilis.

Me

But whacky neighbors, dictators, and Mafiosi aren't the only people with pugilistic *p*'s. They can be found in many people's handwriting, including (gulp) mine!

At least they could have been found in my handwriting, but that's all changed! Years ago, when I was first learning about handwriting profiling, my teacher took one look at my writing and said:

"Michelle, you've sure got a pugilistic *p*, look how high your initial stroke is." "What! No way!" I insisted. "Not me, I absolutely can't have a pugilistic *p*. This time the handwriting has to be wrong!" But alas, as I observed my interactions with others, I noticed that my conversations consisted of everybody talking, nobody listening, and everybody disagreeing afterwards!

up	*up*
impatience	*impatience*
supervisory	*supervisory*
acceptance	*acceptance*
complex	*complex*
My handwriting in 1991	My "new and improved" handwriting now

So I decided to change my handwriting. Every time I wrote, I consciously made my *p* without a high initial stroke. At the same time, I repeated to myself, "I listen when others talk, don't interrupt, and calmly resolve issues." And it worked. As my writing changed, a more gentle, nonconfrontational Michelle emerged. Now when I disagree with people, I'm not nearly as disagreeable.

10

Is That a Phallic Symbol in Your Handwriting or Are You Just Happy to See Me?

These writers share a rather distinctive trait in their handwriting. Can you spot the "sexual symbol" in each of their scripts?

1. The Double Agent; 2. The Prisoner of Perversion; 3. From Kick-Me Kid to Prince of Pain; 4. The Wickedest Man in the World; 5. The Shepherd Who Destroyed His Flock; 6. The Peter of Pan; 7. Wilbur

Freud said, "Sometimes a cigar is just a cigar." But when you see phallus-shaped appendages in a writer's script, it's almost always

114

a sign that the writer is obsessed with sex and has vivid erotic fantasies. Often, these writers can only attain sexual pleasure when indulging in extremely unconventional practices.

The Double Agent

Chevalier d'Éon de Beaumont (known to friends simply as "d'Éon") could have inspired a book called *A Tale of Two Genders*.

Born in 1728, d'Éon was short and chubby, with a gentle, sweet voice. From an early age, d'Éon excelled at languages, politics, and sword fighting. After a brief career as a royal censor, d'Éon joined an elite group of spies under the direct command of King Louis XV. In 1756, the king sent the new recruit on a secret mission to Russia. Posing as the female secretary of a French diplomat, d'Éon obtained a secret audience with Empress Elizabeth. What transpired during their meeting is unknown, but when d'Éon returned to France, the two estranged nations had restored diplomatic relations.

A few years later, d'Éon was dispatched to London to spy on the English. Posing as a diplomat, d'Éon lived large, and largely as a man. D'Éon spent lavishly and became popular with the right sort of people. But others were more circumspect. They wondered if the effeminate envoy was really a woman in disguise. The debate escalated until 300,000 pounds (a "king's ransom" in those days) had been wagered at the London Stock Exchange. The ante was so high that d'Éon feared that he (or she) would be kidnapped, or, even worse, exposed. Still, d'Éon refused to reveal her (or his) gender.

After King Louis XV's death, d'Éon returned to Paris. While in London, d'Éon had acquired secret papers that contained details of a French plan to invade England. D'Éon agreed to turn over the papers if the new king would issue a royal decree publicly announcing d'Éon as a woman. So Louis XVI decreed that d'Éon "was forbidden to appear in any part of our kingdom in any other garments other than those suitable to a female." Along with the order came a generous yearly stipend and money to enable d'Éon to purchase an elaborate wardrobe befitting a lady of his (oops, I mean her) stature. Mademoiselle d'Éon de Beaumont eventually returned to England.

In 1810, the little old lady who was once the talk of two cities, passed away. An autopsy revealed that the mademoiselle, was in fact, a monsieur.

The Prisoner of Perversion

The second writer is Donatien-Alphonse-François, Marquis de Sade (1740–1814). De Sade published detailed descriptions of perverse and cruel—"sadistic"—sexual acts. Some consider his novels celebrations of sexual and political freedom. Unfortunately, many of the acts described in his novels were nonfiction.

De Sade married Renée-Pélagie de Montreuil, the daughter of a wealthy magistrate, in 1763. Her mother thought it was a fair deal: her simple daughter in exchange for de Sade's noble family name. Mme. de Montreuil knew of de Sade's reputation as a "naughty boy," but assumed marriage would tame him. She was wrong. Although she could ignore de Sade's repeated scandals with prostitutes, rumors about his sordid orgies, and his enslavement of young men and women, de Sade's affair with her other (and most favorite) daughter proved too much. Finally, in 1777,

Mme. de Montreuil, whom de Sade called "The Hyena," paid to obtain a "lettre de cachet," a royal decree that allowed the government to imprison an individual without a trial. De Sade spent most of the next two decades in prison and the last thirteen years of his life in an insane asylum, where he continued to scribe his perverse fantasies until the bitter end.

From Kick-Me Kid to Prince of Pain

Leopold von Sacher-Masoch (1836–1895) was to masochism what de Sade was to sadism. As an adult, von Sacher-Masoch described his "supersexual experiences" in two autobiographical novels, the more famous being *Venus in Furs*.

When he was ten, little Leo had a crush on a beautiful countess who used to let the little boy into her boudoir as she dressed. One day the boy was invited to assist the beautiful countess to prepare herself for a liaison. As the boy knelt at her feet, her ermine slippers in his little hands, he suddenly got the urge to kiss her feet. The beautiful countess smiled and responded with a good hard kick, which filled the little masochist with unbridled pleasure.

The Wickedest Man in the World

Aleister Crowley, occultist, poet, and self-described "wickedest man in the world," was a bisexual womanizer and sadist who filed his canine teeth to sharp points so he could bite women like a vampire.

At the beginning of the twentieth century, Crowley created his own religion, based on the "Law of Thelema," which states: "Do what thou wilt shall be the whole of the law." For Crowley, doing what thou wilt meant: "I rave; and I rape and I rip and I rend."

Though his name and signature are probably unfamiliar, you may have seen Crowley's face before. On the cover of the Beatles' *Sgt. Pepper's Lonely Hearts Club Band* LP, Crowley is the rather serious-looking bald chap standing next to Mae West in the back row.

The Shepherd Who Destroyed His Flock

The fifth writer is the Reverend James Warren "Jim" Jones (1931–1978). Jim Jones's mother claimed that before Jim was born a vision came to her and told her that her son would be the messiah.

In the early 1970s Jones was the charismatic leader of the People's Temple.

After former members of the cult complained about Jones's brainwashing and sexual abuse, Jones took 1,000 of his followers to the small country of Guyana in South America, where Jones had built a camp he called Jonestown.

Jones used sex to control his flock. He was their "father" who must be obeyed. All sexual relationships were banned unless they were with him. Jones claimed that having sexual relationships with church members was his "personal sacrifice."

"Of course," wrote one church member, "if they were attractive, he would make the 'sacrifice' sooner rather than later."

Although Jones had been arrested and charged with soliciting sex from a male undercover officer and publicly sodomized a male congregant (as punishment for being a closet homosexual), he preached that he was "the only true heterosexual."

In 1978, Jones ordered his followers to drink a cyanide-laced punch. Over 900 people died, including babies and children (who were forcibly poisoned). Jones shot himself in the head. His dying words were "I tried. I tried. I tried. Mother, Mother. Mother."

The Peter of Pan

Once upon a time, a British documentary crew traveled thousands of miles to interview one of America's most enigmatic pop stars at his California ranch. In a particularly poignant moment, the interviewee exclaimed, in his most gentle, littlest voice: "I am Peter Pan." When asked why he shares his bed with little boys, the pop star replied: "It's not sexual. We're going to sleep. I tuck them in. It's very charming. It's very sweet."

Lawyers and brothers and sisters and mothers and official spokespersons and the ex-wife—who gave up her children and signed a nondisclosure agreement in exchange for an undetermined amount of money and a very nice house—would have you believe that naughty things never never happen in Neverland.

Because Peter Pan would never ever even think of tinkering with Tinker Bell or the children. Right?

Wilbur

Wilbur

You may know Wilbur. He's the guy next door hiding in the bushes with his binoculars, who told his wife he must have left something in his car . . . or the man in the building across the street with the telescope on his balcony, who claims he spends the wee hours tracking a distant star.

If you happen to catch your fiancé with his telescope pointed at the heavenly body in apartment 10B, or your husband takes to wandering around the neighborhood at night in a black lace teddy, or your landlord seems to know far too many details about your personal life . . . should you be concerned?

Have your looked at their handwriting lately?

11

~

Crossing the Line

Come On and Marry Me Bill

On February 14, 1997 a small ad appeared in the *Washington Post*:

HANDSOME

*With love's light wings did
I o'er perch these walls
For stony limits cannot hold love out,
And what love can do that dares love attempt.*
—Romeo and Juliet 2:2

Happy Valentine's Day.

M

On September 11, 1998, at a White House prayer breakfast, Mr. Handsome (aka President Bill Clinton) admitted publicly, "I have sinned." He had denied a relationship with the 22-year-old intern named Monica Lewinsky for months.

Like Romeo and Juliet, Bill and Monica had crossed the line, defied society's rules. Monica went so far as to fall in love with the President, who saw their sexual encounters as a stress reliever. When Bill tried to end their relationship, Monica continued to pursue him.

Do you see how Monica's signature is placed on the far right side of the page, with the lower loop of her *y* literally running off the page? This is a sign of a writer who, like Romeo, against all odds "dares love attempt." Nothing will stop her, not even the edge of the note paper.

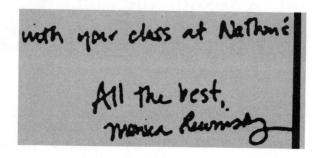

Rule Breakers

One of these writers is a rule breaker. Is it A or B?

A

*Please don't forget to
turn off the oven.
Love,
Mom*

B

All my PENS AND PEN
drawer. MY leTTeRS A.
life saver in Foot locker
socks in LOCKER - WALL - 7

A is my mom Dorothy. She follows the rules.

B is Alberto DeSalvo, the Boston Strangler, whom we met, briefly, in Chapter 7. (Remember the similar strangler strokes in DeSalvo's and Scott Peterson's writing?)

DeSalvo wrote this note in 1969. At that time, DeSalvo was incarcerated and being held for three days in solitary confinement. In the note, DeSalvo was requesting that the prison guard bring him some of his personal belongings from his jail cell.

Do you notice that both my mother and Desalvo wrote on lined paper? My mother began her words after the ruled left margin. However, DeSalvo ignored the ruled left margin and wrote right through it.

The Measuring Man

Two years before Boston was terrorized by the Strangler, a bizarre series of sexual misdemeanors were committed by "the Measuring Man." The Measuring Man would knock on young women's doors and tell them that he was sent by a modeling agency to get their measurements. Flattered, many of the girls complied. The smooth-talking impostor would then whip out a tape measure and get the girls' "vital statistics." After a while, several girls complained to the police.

On March 17, 1961, Cambridge police arrested a man while he was attempting to break into a home. The man confessed to committing numerous burglaries. He also volunteered that he was the Measuring Man. He explained his motivation for measuring to the detectives: "I'm not good looking. I'm not educated, but I was able to put something over on high-class people. They were all college kids and I never had anything in my life and I outsmarted them."

Paroled after eighteen months, the Measuring Man transformed himself into a much more dangerous offender, known as the Green Man. The Green Man—so named because he wore green work clothes—was arrested for breaking into an apartment. He had tied a young woman to her bed, sexually assaulted her, and then, before leaving, apologized. A sketch artist drew the Green Man's face based on the woman's description. The Green Man, detectives realized, was their old friend, the Measuring Man, aka Alberto DeSalvo.

Here's another sample of DeSalvo's writing. Take a look at the *E* in "East" (the word to the right of the letters *B.t.*). Notice how it creeps downward, crossing below the baseline. When letters drop below the baseline, where they normally shouldn't be, it's another sign that the writer ignores society's rules. Writers whose letters lurk below the baseline are almost always sneaky types who hide behind a facade or create a ruse to conceal their true motives.

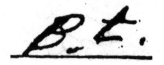

Instant Replay

Now let's focus on the initials *B.t.* Can you see how DeSalvo repetitively wrote over the lines of the letters? When a writer goes over and over letters, it's a sign of a compulsive neurotic, someone who will overindulge in sex, drugs, or alcohol to alleviate built up tension and angst.

Irmgard, DeSalvo's wife, claimed that her husband had an insatiable sexual appetite, wanting sex at least six times a day.

Albert DeSalvo seemed to relish being in the spotlight, at one point selling "Boston Strangler Choker Chains" from his jail cell. But was DeSalvo the Boston Strangler, as he had claimed? We will never know for sure, but one thing is certain, as the Measuring Man and the Green Man, Albert DeSalvo crossed the line many times. Nothing could stop this sex-obsessed rule-breaker from acting out his sick fantasies—nothing except his own big mouth.

The Mastermind

As you've seen, when letter structures fall below the established baseline, the writer may appear to be above board, but below the surface he is furiously scheming and planning.

This is the signature of Mohamed Atta. Do you see that a section of his name plunges below the baseline?

Guest Signature

Mohamed Atta, one of the principal hijackers involved in the crash of American Airlines Flight 11 into the north tower of the World Trade Center, had been secretly preparing for the attack for years. In 1999, Atta organized an Islamic prayer group at the student union of the Technical University Hamburg-Harburg. It is now believed that the group was a front to recruit students to his fanatical cause. In July of 2000, he learned to fly an aircraft in Venice, Florida.

Atta led a sleeper cell in the United States for two years, operating under the radar.

With your left hand, cover every letter except for the *d* in the name "Mohamed." Can you tell that the *d* is in fact a *d*? When you isolate the *d,* you can't tell what it is. When lowercase *d*'s are distorted to the point of being unrecognizable, it is a sign of a writer with warped personal values. This includes ideas, morals, beliefs, and lifestyle.

It probably won't surprise you to learn that Atta's handwriting also reveals narrow-mindedness, a trait common to fundamentalists. Look at the pinched narrow pointed top of the letter *A* in Atta. Remember that the upper zone represents what's going on in the head. Atta's tightly squished upper zone is a clear indication of his restricted thinking and his closed mind.

NARROW MINDED PEOPLE THINK ALIKE

In the 1950s, Senator Joe McCarthy led the US Senate Permanent Subcommittee on Investigations, which destroyed the reputations and careers of many good people based on rumors and accusations of past "un-American activities."

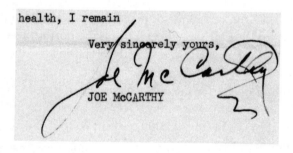

The pointy top of the *J* in Senator Joe McCarthy's signature—like Atta's pointy *A*—reflects his narrow-mindedness.

The Secret Society

What do these three writers have in common?

A

B

C

Answer: like a secret handshake, these three writers share a common trait in their handwriting. Notice that each writing sample has at least one ending stroke that crossed the line.

I call this the "lurking lunatic stroke." These writers are stealthy, sneaky, and secretive. They tend to be loners who are practiced in revealing little if nothing of themselves or their plans to others.

By the way, our lunatic crew has something else in common: each of these writers planned secretly to assassinate an American president.

The first assassin is Charles Guiteau. On July 2, 1881, President James A. Garfield arrived at Washington's Baltimore & Potomac train station to board a train to the Jersey shore. Lurking in a corner of the waiting room was Charles Guiteau.

In this sample, the ending stroke of the *e* in "Blame" drops sharply below the baseline.

Guiteau was a failed journalist, attorney, and revivalist preacher who moved frequently to avoid paying his rent and elude his many creditors. As a Garfield supporter, Guiteau was sure that Garfield's election would be the lucky break he needed. When he received no reply to his personal letter to the President requesting a position as the American consul-general in Vienna, he wrote again, confessing that he really would much prefer Paris. "I presume my appointment will be promptly confirmed," he wrote. When again, no reply was forthcoming, Guiteau turned to Plan C.

As the President and his entourage passed by, Guiteau fired two shots. President Garfield technically did not die from Guiteau's bullet. Rather, he lingered for an agonizing two and a half months, suffering from an infection that his doctors had given him when they pried the bullet out of his back with their bare unclean hands and dirty surgical instruments.

Assassin #2 is Leon Czolgosz. During a meet-and-greet at the Pan American Exposition in Buffalo, New York, President William McKinley reached out to shake a hand in the crowd. As the President extended his hand toward him, a 28-year-old anarchist named Leon Czolgosz fired two shots point blank into McKinley's midsection. One deflected off a button. The other nicked the President's liver. McKinley died a few days later. Czolgosz confessed it was "his duty" to kill the President.

Czolgosz had been secretly planning an assassination for some time. In his pocket, police found an article about the assassination of King Umberto in Italy by an anarchist named Gaetano Bresci. However, Czolgosz was such a loner that other anarchists were suspicious of him. Something about him made them suspect he might be a spy.

Notice how the *e* in "me" and *h* in "much" cross down past the baseline.

In his early twenties, assassin #3, son of a workaholic oil tycoon and his agoraphobic wife, was obsessed with actress Jodie Foster and her movie *Taxi Driver*. He began living a secret fantasy life based on the film. He dropped out of college and drifted around the country, eventually moving to New Haven, Connecticut, where he began stalking Jodie Foster, then a student at Yale. He wrote Foster poems and letters, confessing his undying love, and, lurking in the shadows, observed Foster from afar.

Notice how the *e* in Hinckley's "me" dips downward, below the line.

After months of quietly lurking by chamber doors, Hinckley was ready to leap. On March 29, 1981, Hinckley checked into the Park Central Hotel in Washington, DC, ready to carry out his secret plan. On the morning of March 30, Hinckley had breakfast at McDonald's, took a Valium, and wrote another desperate letter to Jodie:

"Jodie, I would abandon this idea of getting Reagan in a second if I could only win your heart and live out the rest of my life with you, whether it be in total obscurity or whatever."

It was a short cab ride to the Washington Hilton. Observers

remember a voice calling out: "President Reagan, President Reagan!" As President Reagan turned toward the voice, Hinckley fired six shots in rapid succession, wounding Reagan, his press secretary James Brady, and two others. John Hinckley, found not guilty by reason of insanity, is living in a mental hospital in Washington, DC.

12

⌒

Tick . . . Tick . . . Tick . . .

Are you a ticking time bomb? Of course, you're always calm, cool, and collected. Though, on occasion, you do drive a bit too aggressively. And remember that snide remark you made to the woman in front of you who had forty-two items in the express checkout aisle?

Before you run out and sign up for anger management classes, here's a little test.

Get out a pen and paper and write the following question:

> If Peter Piper picked a peck of pickled peppers,
> how many pickled peppers did Peter Piper pick?

Did you do it? (Just checking) Put the paper aside for now. We'll see how you did later.

Only When He Drinks

Gloria from Hackensack's having a problem with her husband:

> My husband and I have been having serious troubles. We are fighting and I simply do not know what to do.
> When Jack drinks, he gets so angry he'll put his fists through doors. Several times, he has actually waved loaded guns around. I needed to call the police to calm him down.

After the gun incidents and a few other awful fights, I told him to move out, take his dog and leave me alone.

Jack moved out, got his own place, and started AA meetings and "recovery." After six months of separation, we started to see each other and he seemed much calmer. I wanted to believe that he was "better." So we moved back in with each other.

People think he's a good catch because I have a big house, nice car, work for myself out of my home, have nice things and so on. But, something is not right. It doesn't take much to send him into a rage and I never know what will set him off.

Below is a sample of Jack's handwriting. Notice anything unusual about his punctuation? This writer went over his punctuation marks again and again, grinding them into the paper. We call these heavy, dark periods and *i* dots "explosive dots."

When you see so many explosive dots in a writer's script, they are a sign of a writer who is angry, irritable, and obsessive.

Show me an alcoholic with a bad temper, and I'll show you a writer who grinds his dots. He may also grind his teeth, but that's another story.

Now, look closely at the letter *c* in "could" and the *P* in "Please." Do they remind you of anything—an animal, perhaps? (Hint: I call these formations "coiled strokes.") Writers with coiled strokes are like snakes—wound up and ready to strike without warning.

Good catch? I don't know. With those explosive dots and coiled strokes, I'd throw this big fish back in the sea.

The Junk Yard

Recently Jenny faxed me a letter. It seems her head was spinning after she tried to help a friend:

> I'm hoping that you can help me understand a guy I know (or thought I knew). I've been friends with Stewart for several years. He is an attorney. Last week, his secretary got sick and had to go to the hospital. He called and said that he had a load of work and asked me to help him. When I got to his office he screamed for hours about his secretary, saying stuff like, "that bleeping fat stupid bleep." His face turned bright red. I told him to calm down and that I couldn't help him if he continued to act crazy. He went into his office and slammed his door. That night he called and apologized.
>
> The next day he called and said that his secretary was still sick. I arranged for my cousin to help him. He called me around 11 AM and said that my cousin had just gotten up and walked out.
>
> "What did you say to her?" I asked. "Are you saying it's my fault?" he screamed. He hung up on me. I called back and he hung up again.

Do you see how the *S* in Stewart begins with a straight, unbending line? That's a resentment stroke. It shows that it's hard for Stewart to "let go." Once he gets worked up, he begins wrapping another rubber band around the big rubber ball—the ever growing sum of all the "injustices" he's had to endure in his life.

Stewart

When you see words with long, straight lead-in strokes that start at or below the baseline, the writer is carrying around a lot of junk from the past. This stroke shows up in the handwriting of people who have elephant-like memories and extremely thin hides. When things don't go their way, they blame everyone but themselves. They are often combative and angry, and can hold a grudge.

The longer, heavier, and more frequent are resentment strokes in a script, the deeper the writer's bitterness and anger. In extreme cases the deep-rooted resentment can explode into a violent rage.

The resentment strokes in Stewart's handwriting are light and short. So while he may get his briefs in a twist over seemingly little things, Stewart is not likely to "go postal." Nonetheless, if Stewart asked me to help around the office, I'd tell him to call a temp service.

Like Mother Like Son

In Chapter 5, you met Sante Kimes, arsonist, con artist, slave master. Now meet her son Kenny.

> Living with my mother and brother was like living with a time bomb strapped to my back. I was surrounded by wealth and comfort but knew something very bad was about to happen.
>
> > Kent Walker, writing about his mother,
> > Sante Kimes, and half-brother, Kenny Kimes,
> > in *Son of a Grifter: The Twisted Tale*
> > *of Sante and Kenny Kimes, the Most*
> > *Notorious Con Artists in America*

Since he was a tyke, Kenny's mother had encouraged him to cheat, lie, and steal. When Kenny got caught stealing a surfboard as a young teenager, Sante was furious. "I don't care if you steal anything," she yelled, "just don't be so stupid as to get caught, you fucking idiot!"

Manhattan socialite Irene Silverman was immediately impressed with 23-year-old "Manny Guerrin." Manny (aka Kenny Kimes) drove a Lincoln Town Car, wore a beautiful suit, and carried a big wad of cash. He seemed to know the right people, and all the right things to say. So Silverman, an outgoing, 82-year-old widow who rented out suites in her Upper East Side mansion for $6,000 a month, welcomed the young man into her home.

But almost immediately, she sensed that something wasn't right. Who was the middle-aged woman who moved into Manny's suite, claiming to be his "assistant"? What was going on behind closed doors?

Silverman confided to her friend Janice Herbert, "I have this tenant who is driving all of us crazy! We can't get into the room to clean, and I suspect he's hiding something in there. He's not nice, and he's rude, and I suspect that something very bad is going on."

Ten days later, on July 5, 1998, Irene Silverman disappeared.

"Kenny, be careful," Sante shrieked. "Yes, Momma," Kenny replied quietly. Little red drops were dribbling out of the heavy duffel bag onto the Manhattan sidewalk as Kenny lugged it toward the stolen green Lincoln Town Car.

Sante helped Kenny stuff Mrs. Silverman into the trunk.

"Whew, that was quite a load," Sante said, as she gave Kenny a hug and a big kiss on the lips. Quickly, the mother and son team got into the green car. As Kenny pressed his foot on the gas, Sante brushed the hair away from his face. "Momma told you we could do it. Didn't she?"

Just a few hours after disposing of Silverman's body, Sante and Kenny were picked up by the FBI, and arrested on a Utah warrant for a bad check. It was the check Sante had used to buy the green Lincoln Town Car. Authorities knew nothing about Mrs. Silverman's disappearance, and the Kimeses volunteered nothing.

However, in the stolen Lincoln, police found handcuffs, hypodermic needles, out-of-state license plates, a loaded pistol, Irene Silverman's passport with Sante Kimes's picture, a forged bill of sale for the Silverman mansion, and thirteen notebooks in Sante Kimes's handwriting. The notebooks contained every detail of the plot to murder Irene Silverman and steal her townhouse.

In the trash outside Silverman's mansion, investigators dug up an envelope with Kenny's scribbled handwriting and doodles. On the envelope Kenny had doodled images of teacups, cubes, and coffins. In addition, he had written the words "Silverman," "Blood," and "Bleeding."

Let's look at just two words:

In the word "Bleeding," notice the letters *l* and *e*. The *l* could be an *s*, *x*, *h*, or maybe a *k*. The *e* could be an *o* or an *a*. Kenny learned well from his momma—he's a consummate con artist who wants you to see what he wants you to see. Remember, when you find a writer who makes letters or numbers that are ambiguous and disguised, you are almost certainly looking at someone who is deceptive.

Also, notice that "Bleeding" is missing a letter. Assuming that Kenny can spell the word correctly, the missing letter shows that he skims over the truth and leaves out important details.

Now look at the word "Blood." The ink fills the oval in the second *o* and the oval in the letter *d*. These blotched patches of excessive ink show a person with excessive and uncontrollable needs. Sexual urges and intrusive thoughts fill Kenny's muddied head. Take a good look at the letter *d* in "Blood." See how it ends thickly and bluntly like a club? Yes, that is our old friend, the club stroke, the mark of a cruel and brutal person. And finally, notice how Kenny slashes his dot above the *i* in "Bleeding." Slashed dots are a sign of a person with a short fuse and a hot temper. Poor Irene Silverman—taking in a tenant with club strokes, blotched ovals, disguised letters, and slashed *i* dots— didn't stand a chance.

At their arraignment in a Manhattan courtroom, mother and son appeared close, too close. "Mommy and Clyde," as the tabloids called them, couldn't stop looking at each other, squeezing and holding hands. "Would you please stop doing that?" asked the annoyed judge.

Although Irene Silverman's body was never found, the Kimeses were convicted of her murder and more than fifty other crimes. Sante and Kenny stood together as they were sentenced to a total of 245 years behind bars.

A few months after their separation and confinement, Kenny, desperate to prevent his mother from being extradited to California to stand trial for another murder, wrote this letter to Court TV reporter Maria Zone inviting her to interview him in prison.

Look at the *i* dots in this note. Slashes here, slashes there, slashes everywhere. Yes, those slashes show that Kenny is frustrated and irritable, but slashed *i* dots can show something else. You will also find slashed *i* dots in the handwriting of people who like to use sharp objects as weapons—a lesson that Maria Zone was soon about to learn.

Zone agreed to interview Kenny at the Clinton Correction Facility in upstate New York. Thirty minutes into the interview, Kenny grabbed Maria Zone's pen. Then he grabbed Maria and held the pen to her neck. "This is a hostage situation. This is a hostage situation," Kenny shouted.

Four hours later, negotiators were able to distract Kenny and wrestle him to the ground. Zone was shaken up but not hurt. Kenneth Kimes was put in solitary confinement for eight years.

Tick Marks

A chapter titled "Tick . . . Tick . . . Tick . . ." certainly wouldn't be complete without telling you about "ticks." A tick mark is a little checkmark-like stroke at the beginning or end of a letter. Tick mark writers will throw a temper tantrum at the drop of a Tic-Tac. Tick marks are signs of rage, antagonism, irritability, and frustration.

Do you see the checkmark in Hitler's signature? That is a tick mark.

Dennis Nilsen was considerate to a fault. Even those he tried to strangle in their sleep recalled how polite he had been to them. But Dennis Nilsen's handwriting shows that inside the shell of this mild-mannered civil servant was a monster seething with rage.

Take a good look at Nilsen's handwriting. Do you see that almost every word starts with an angular check mark? These frequent ticks in Nilsen's handwriting show that he's seething mad—like a hot cauldron ready to boil over. And yet his handwriting is very controlled and even. The combination of these two elements shows that Nilsen is very angry and frustrated, but rarely shows his anger to others.

When Dennis was seven, his father abandoned the family. Olav Nilsen, an alcoholic Norwegian sailor, hadn't been around much anyway. After his parents divorced, his mother remarried and started a new family. Dennis felt invisible next to his four new siblings. But Dennis was a good, quiet boy. If he was angry or pained, it never showed. At sixteen, he joined the army and worked as a cook. In the army, Nilsen kept to himself. He drank heavily, and began to fantasize about having sex with boys.

In 1972, after eleven years in the army, he retired and moved to London. He was twenty-seven. After training to be a policeman, Nilsen worked as a job counselor in a government employment office. On weekends, the mild-mannered civil servant trawled pubs for young male companions.

Nilsen rented a ground floor flat in North London. One of its nicest features was that it had a garden. For a time, he lived there with a flat mate. Then, one night, after a blow-up, he ordered his flat mate to leave. Lonely, and socially isolated, he began to drink more heavily.

Nilsen wanted a new flat mate. One night, he picked up a young man in a pub and took him back to the flat. As Nilsen stared intently at the sleeping body next to him in his bed, he thought, "In a few hours, he's going to leave me and I'll be alone again."

Then he slipped a necktie around the man's neck and pulled tightly. When the man awoke and started to fight back, Nilsen fought harder. After the life drained out of the man, Nilsen washed his body in the bathroom, and dragged it back into his bed. He found it comforting to talk to the corpse.

An interesting feature of Nilsen's handwriting is the openness of his communication letters. Notice how his o's and a's are open at the top. As we saw in Chapter 5, this is a sign of a talker. Dennis Nilsen loved to talk. He just preferred to talk to people after he killed them.

When he finished chitchatting with his victim, he stuffed the corpse in the crawl space under the floorboards in his living room. A week later, he pulled the body out and washed it again. He found the rotting flesh beautiful and sexy. And when he felt lonely, he had someone to talk to. "It was the beginning of the end of my life as I had known it," he later wrote. "I had started down the avenue of death and possession of a new kind of flat mate."

Eventually, Nilsen would dispose of his new flat mates in the garden, piece by piece. No one ever asked him what it was that he was burning.

In 1982, when Nilsen moved into a new building, he left the remains of twelve men behind. His new apartment was in an attic.

There was no garden or crawl space. Nilsen thought that if he changed his living arrangements he could stop killing. But soon the attic flat began to fill up with suitcases. There were body parts in the bathroom and kitchen cupboards, too.

One day, the toilets in his building backed up, and the owner called in a plumber. The plumber found there was something unusual blocking the drains. The blockage appeared to be pieces of human flesh.

When the detectives asked Nilsen about the drains he calmly invited them into his flat, showed them the suitcases and plastic bags that contained the rest of the body parts, and began to talk and talk and talk (as you would expect of a writer with communication letters that are open at the top).

In sickening detail he told police how he had killed and mutilated fifteen men and attempted, but failed, to kill seven others. He even helped police identify parts of his victims.

At his trial, those "flat mates" who were lucky enough to walk out the door testified that they had left Nilsen's apartment with bruises and strange red marks on their throats. A few said they thought they were having a bad dream, a nightmare. In the nightmare, an enraged killer was trying to strangle them. But when they awoke, hung over and sore, Nilsen was bright and cheery. One morning, he asked a man he had just tried to strangle and drown during the night for a second date.

In 1983, the judge sentenced Nilsen to life in prison, where Nilsen continues to write and talk profusely. He told one reporter: "I caused dreams, which inevitably caused death. This is my crime. I wished I could stop, but I could not. I had no other thrill or happiness."

A Very Bad Sign

In the late 1960s and early 1970s, the Zodiac killer murdered more than thirty-five people in the San Francisco Bay area. He taunted the police with notes that described how his next victim would be killed. Sometimes he included a piece of his victim's bloodstained clothing in the envelope. While the Zodiac was able to keep his identity secret, he didn't want to go unnoticed, either. This killer had a huge ego. You can see this in his large personal pronoun "I."

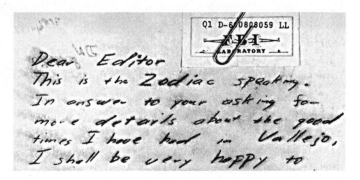

In fact, the Zodiac's ego was so large that when the police got details of his crimes wrong, he would get upset and write them scolding letters.

But there's something else in the Zodiac's handwriting that tells his tale. Look carefully again at the note. Many of the individual letters lean far to the right. But one letter in particular falls drastically rightward. Which letter is it?

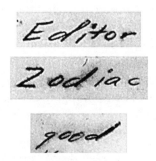

If you guessed the letter *d,* give yourself a gold star.

This writer's hand suddenly collapsed to the right as he wrote the letter *d,* forming a stroke known as the dreaded "diabolical *d.*" When the lower case *d* leans far to right, relative to the rest of a writer's script, it's a sign of someone who is unpredictable and prone to extreme emotional outbursts. Writers with diabolical *d*'s in their script may want others to see them as big shots but they actually have fragile egos and can easily become defensive. They may be able to control their tempers for a while, but you can never know when they'll trip up—like their collapsed *d*'s—and fall off the deep end.

As mysteriously and suddenly as they had started, the string of Zodiac murders that terrified Northern California stopped. The Zodiac killer has never been identified or apprehended.

Water Pistol or Nuclear Missile?

Take out the handwriting sample that you wrote at the beginning of the chapter ("If Peter Piper picked a peck of pickled peppers, how many pickled peppers did Peter Piper pick?")

Let's look at your *i* dots. If you made your dots plain, light, and rounded, usually you can keep your temper in check. However, if your dots are slashed and dashed, then you can get mighty irritable. And if you made your *i* dots or punctuation marks excessively heavy and ground-in, you are obsessive, tense, and resentful, and can lose your temper at the drop of a hat.

A. The explosive dots of David Berkowitz, aka "Son of Sam"; B. The slashed dots of Kenneth Kimes; C. The heavy, ground-in dots of the Zodiac killer

If you were feeling testy when you took the test, you probably made a few tick marks on the first letters of some of your words. If you made a lot of tick marks, it may be time to take stock, get help, or sign up for a few years of yoga classes.

Does your writing show resentment? If some of your words begin with long, straight lead-in strokes that start at or below the baseline, you may have some resentment about people and events in your past. Psychotherapy can sometimes help you understand why you're so resentful and help you work through your feelings. On the other hand, Sigmund Freud spent years working through his issues, and his handwriting shows huge resentment strokes.

So how do you rate yourself on the explosive temper scale? Water pistol or nuclear missile?

PART III

The Forensic Files

13

Bad to the Bone

Sometimes the killer will leave a note at the scene of a crime, or write letters to the press or police. This is where a handwriting profiler comes in.

An accurate profile can be an invaluable tool in an investigation. Criminal profiling is used to narrow down an investigation to those suspects who possess certain behavioral and personality traits. The profile enables investigators to refine their suspect list and target their resources where they might be the most useful.

Another valuable use of a profile is to generate leads. By involving the public in crime solving, the hope is that someone will recognize the unknown suspect from the profile and come forward with information.

You Are the Profiler

Here's the scenario: You are a junior detective in a big city police department. You have been assigned to a police task force created to catch a suspected serial killer. Over the last several years, coeds have been disappearing from college campuses. The bones of one of the missing girls have been found scattered in a forest.

One eyewitness reported seeing a man speeding away from the campus in a car with a woman matching the description of one of the missing coeds. She thinks the car may have been green, or tan, or maybe it was yellow. It had two doors or it was a station wagon. It was either Japanese or German, or maybe an American car. Not much to go on.

But one of the missing coed's roommates has found a hand-written note on a napkin under the couch. Tests reveal that there were blood splatters on the napkin that matched the blood type of the missing girl. A team of psychologists is analyzing the note's contents for clues. This morning, your commander gave you the task of building a profile of the unidentified subject (the UNSUB) based on the handwriting in the note. Your profile could be the key to identifying and apprehending the UNSUB.

What can you tell about the author of this note from his hand-writing?

BUILDING A PROFILE
1. At first glance, does this handwriting look normal or abnormal? Crude or refined? Do you think the UNSUB will physically look rough and tattered or blend in with the norm?
2. Is the UNSUB highly educated or a high-school dropout?

3. Does the handwriting slant to the left or the right? Is the UNSUB a social person? Does he lean toward people or away from people?

4. Is the writing fairly large or is it teeny-weeny? Is the UNSUB outgoing or withdrawn? Would you be more likely to find our suspect around other people or hidden alone and isolated in a hut in the woods?

5. Is any zone exaggerated or distorted? If so, what could that mean?

6. Study the personal pronoun "I." What kind of relationship do you think the UNSUB had with his mother? What about his father?

7. Do you see any signs of anger or resentment?

8. Look at the first sentence. Do you see anything odd about the letter *f* in the word "for" and the letter *b* in the word "October"?

9. Any signs that our UNSUB is the type of person who ignores rules and "crosses the line"? (Hint: Check out the first word in the first sentence.)

10. And finally, study the word "living." What the heck is that on the bottom of the letter *l*?

PULLING IT TOGETHER

1. At first glance this handwriting looks more or less normal. Unlike the handwriting of someone like Charles Manson, which has ugly doodles and swastikas throughout the script, this writing isn't initially crude or "crazy looking." So unlike Charles Manson, who is a bizarre-looking man with a swastika tattooed on his forehead, our UNSUB—like his handwriting—won't look out of the ordinary.

2. The writing has a nice smooth flow, no misspellings, and most of the letters are well formed. This shows that our UNSUB is probably refined and well educated.

3. The writing leans to the right. Our UNSUB will lean toward people.

4. The writing is fairly large. Our writer is relatively outgoing. Our UNSUB will mingle well with others. He doesn't like to be isolated. We will most likely find him living and interacting with other people.

5. The lower zone is exaggerated. See how the extra large loop of the *y* in the word "you" extends into the word "Graham" in the line underneath it? The loop of the *y* invades the upper zone of the letter *G*, intrudes through the middle zone and creeps past the lower zone. In fact, his lower zone is so exaggerated that it not only violates the line underneath it, it actually penetrates the handwriting two lines below. Do you think our UNSUB, a man who writes with lower zones like these, can stay within society's sexual boundaries? Absolutely not.

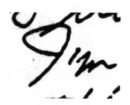

6. The mother stroke is huge and distorted. The father stroke is nonexistent. Most likely the mother figure played a prominent role in our UNSUB's life, though the relationship between the mother and son may have been unclear or distorted. The father played little or no role in our UNSUB's life.

7. With all those long, heavy resentment strokes, our UNSUB has been holding anger in for many years. When our UNSUB lets his anger out he will explode with a vengeance.

8. That *f* and *b* are the good old phallic symbol. Our UNSUB can get his kicks sexually only in a bizarre and abnormal manner.

9. The *T* in the word "Thanks" drops under the baseline. Our UNSUB definitely crosses the line and is adept at being sneaky.

10. This is the same little pitchfork, or devil's fork, we saw in the signatures of Keith Jesperson (the Happy Face killer) and Dennis Rader (the BTK killer). The killer believes that the devil made him do it.

The UNSUB

From a single handwriting sample, we were able to build a detailed profile of the UNSUB. But does the profile fit?

As you may have guessed, the note we just examined was not written on a cocktail napkin. This particular handwriting sample is from a letter written by convicted serial killer Ted Bundy. Bundy abducted and killed at least thirty-six women in the mid-1970s. Only Bundy knew the exact number of his victims.

On January 24, 1989, 42-year-old Ted Bundy was executed in the electric chair by the State of Florida for the murder of Kimberly Leach.

Let's see how our profile compares to Bundy.

Does the Profile Fit?

1. The UNSUB appears "normal."

Bundy was well groomed and refined looking. Most people who met him described him as quite handsome. In fact he was such a "poster boy" that the Washington State Republican Party hired him.

2. The UNSUB is well educated.

Before he enrolled at the University of Utah Law School, Bundy attended Stanford University on a scholarship in Chinese studies and graduated with honors in psychology.

3. The UNSUB leans toward people.

Bundy was charming, witty, and friendly. He played tennis, served as a suicide prevention volunteer, and joined the Seattle Crime Prevention Council.

4. The UNSUB doesn't like to be isolated. We will find him living and mingling with people.

Bundy's favorite place to live was on or near college campuses.

5. The UNSUB cannot stay within society's sexual boundaries.

Bundy had an uncontrollable urge to torture, rape, and kill women. Even after his victims had suffocated or bled to death, Bundy continued to sexually assault them.

6. The UNSUB had a relationship with his mother; however, it was distorted. His father played little or no role in his life.

Bundy spent the first four months of his life in an orphanage. Afterwards, he went to live with his mother, father (whom distant relatives called mean and crazy), and an older sister. When Bundy was four years old his teenage sister took him with her and moved to another state. In his mid-twenties, Bundy decided to research his birth records. While researching his birth records, Bundy got quite a surprise. He discovered that his "sister" was actually his mother and the people he thought were his parents were actually his grandparents. Ted never knew his biological father.

7. The UNSUB has deep-rooted resentment. When he lets out his anger, he will explode with a vengeance.

When his first serious girlfriend broke up with him in college, he was devastated. Years later, he would plot to win her back, only to cruelly reject her so that she would feel the same pain she had caused him. Though outwardly Bundy was a successful young Republican, active in politics and the community, inside Ted Bundy was still seething with anger and resentment for past hurts.

Bundy's resentment grew after he learned the truth about his parentage. Shortly after this discovery, he began a rampage that led to the brutal rapes and torture of at least thirty-six young women.

8. Our UNSUB can only get sexual pleasure in abnormal or bizarre ways.

Bundy raped, bit, and sexually tortured his victims before, during, and after he killed them. He later blamed pornography for making him lose control of his sexual urges.

9. The UNSUB crosses the line and is adept at being sneaky.

While Bundy was imprisoned in Aspen awaiting his trial, he convinced the warden to let him study in the law library, where he proceeded to climb out the window, jump twenty feet, and flee. Eight days later he was apprehended while trying to leave town in a stolen car.

Seven months later, he escaped again. After months of near-starvation, Bundy had lost thirty pounds. He unscrewed the light fixture in the ceiling of his cell at Garfield County Jail, and slithered through the crawl space. He ended up in the closet of the warden's apartment. He waited there until nobody was around and then calmly walked out the front door. No one noticed that Bundy was missing for over fifteen hours. By then, he was on his way to Tallahassee, Florida.

10. The UNSUB believed that the devil was inside of him.

On death row, Ted Bundy assisted the FBI in developing a profile of the Green River killer in his home state of Washington. He also developed a number of theories about his own psychology. He claimed that he didn't mean to kill, blaming an evil "entity" within him for his unspeakable actions.

On a Personal Note

I got the idea for this scenario from Joan, a woman I met at one of my lectures. After asking me to "do her handwriting," the short, round, gray-haired woman told me a little story about herself.

"Thirty years ago," she said, "I met a handsome man in a coffee shop. He passed me a note, written on a napkin, asking me for a date."

She cleared her throat. "After evaluating the situation, I decided to decline the gentleman's offer." She hesitated for a moment. "About two years later, I saw the man's picture in the paper. He had been arrested in Florida. That man, the man from the coffee shop, was Ted Bundy."

I asked her, "Did you see something in his writing? Was it the large lower loops in his script that scared you off? Did you see that devil's fork? Or was it all those long resentment strokes?"

"No," Joan answered. "The truth is, at that time in my life, I didn't feel very good about myself. If a good-looking guy made a pass at me, I thought, 'What's he interested in me for?'" "You know," she confided, "I was never what you would call a beauty."

I glanced down at her writing and noticed that her personal pronoun "I" was teeny.

Handwriting profiling is a tool that can be amazingly accurate in predicting behavior. But who could have predicted that Joan's low self-esteem would save her life?

14

~

The Devil's in the Details

Here are two cases for you to ponder. I'll give you some background information, a few clues, and some handwriting samples. What can you tell about these two subjects from their scripts?

Case 1: Can She Trust Him With Her Heart?

An attractive blonde shows up at your door with a handwriting sample and a question. "Should I marry this man?"

She explains, "He's thirty and I'm twenty-seven. My girlfriend fixed us up on a blind date. I haven't known him too long, but I really like him. He's handsome, funny, ambitious, and charming. And he's so romantic! The conversation just flows so well between us, but . . ."

She pauses for a minute and then adds, "He told me he had never been married. Then, last weekend, we had this talk about trust. Like, 'How do I know I can trust you?' And then he told me that he had lost his wife . . . that he had been married, but she died. And he looked so sad, like a hurt little puppy . . . So I need to know . . ."

"What?" you ask.

"I want to know . . . can I trust this man with my heart?"

Here's his handwriting. What will you tell her?

GARY

WE ARE IN RECEIPT OF INVOICE #
① WE HAVE NOT SENT PAYMENT FOR
AS WE FEEL SOME ADJUSTMENT
FOR THE POOR QUALITY FINISH C
IMMEDIATELY SURROUNDING THE T
NOTABLY TRAVEL MARKS, BACK
POOR FINISH ON EDGE, ETC

PLEASE CONSIDER AN ADJUSTMENT
ASAP. PLEASE UTILIZE MAIL FOR

THANK YOU,

If you take a superficial look at this script you might think, "This letter looks neat, normal, and readable." And most likely, the young woman's boyfriend would give a nice impression. He would also look neat, normal, and quite presentable. A surface view would make you believe that you could easily understand and "read" this man. But let's look beyond our first impressions.

On first glance, this letter seems easy to read. But is it? Remember from Chapter 5 that if you meet someone who writes with ambiguous letters or trick numbers, you are almost always dealing with a trickster or a con artist.

Let's look at a few words and numbers from this letter taken out of context:

96351 PAYMENT QUALITY CONSIDER BACK
MARKS IN ARE INVOICE SURROUNDING ON
ADJUSTMENT SENT THE THIS SOME MAIL

Without context to help us, this writing is not very readable, is it? This writer is a pro at making you see what he wants you to see.

Maybe sometimes distance does make the heart grow fonder, but when you see distance in a lover's script, it's a sign of a lonely achin' heart. Notice the abnormally wide spaces between the words. This overly wide spacing shows that this writer wants to put space between himself and others. This sort of writing is typical of people who have a deep fear of intimacy.

This letter was written by Scott Peterson on June 24, 2002, five months before his first date with Amber Frey. Amber thought of Scott as her "boyfriend." She had no idea that Scott was married and that his wife Laci was pregnant with their first child.

On December 9, 2002, Scott told Amber that he was a widower and the sad story of how his wife had died. A few weeks later, on Christmas Eve, his wife disappeared.

In April 2003, Laci Peterson's badly decomposed torso and the body of her unborn child washed onto a beach two miles north of Berkeley, California. Scott Peterson was arrested near San Diego as he was preparing to flee the country.

In his red Mercedes, investigators found four cell phones, nearly $15,000 in cash, survival gear (including a water purifier), duct tape, three knives, and a bottle of Viagra. Peterson was also carrying a MapQuest printout (downloaded earlier that same day) of directions to American Bodyworks, the Fresno massage studio where Amber Frey worked.

In December 2004, a jury found Scott Peterson guilty of the first degree murder of Laci and their baby. During the trial's penalty phase, Scott Peterson's older half-brother pleaded to the jury that Scott was a kind and loving man and that there was no way Scott could have murdered Laci. But prosecutors painted a different picture of Scott. He was, they said, a pathological liar who coldly planned this murder as a way of freeing himself from the burden of a wife and child and enabling him to pursue his relationship with Amber.

Case 2: The Hitchhiker

You see a hitchhiker by the side of the road. You never pick up hitchhikers. But today, for some reason, you feel compelled to stop. However, as a precaution, you ask the hitchhiker for a writing sample. You roll down your window just enough to slip the hitchhiker a pad and pen. After looking very carefully at this sample of the hitchhiker's script, you feel a shudder down your spine. "Keep the pen," you holler, as you step on the accelerator, leaving the hitchhiker in a cloud of dust.

Your little handwriting test may have saved your life.

Here's the hitchhiker's writing. It looks so nice and neat.

What was it about this script that caused you to put your pedal to the metal?

1. The handwriting is perfect—too perfect. Writing that is too tight, too controlled, and too pretty shows that the writer is compensating for an inner feeling of loss of control. Overly controlled writers are unpredictable and often volatile. Everything may seem hunky-dory until one day when something sets them off. And when these overly controlled writers do go off, watch out, because when they lose control they really lose control!

2. In English-speaking cultures, we write from left to right. Therefore, the left side of the page (where we begin) represents

our past while the right side (where we're going) represents our future. The extra wide left side margin in the note shows that this hitchhiker wants to move far away from the past.

3. A person's personal pronoun "I" often reveals information about the writer's background. The vertical loop represents the mother figure, while the horizontal loop represents the father figure. Both loops of this writer's personal pronoun are tight and squeezed. The *I* also starts with a resentment stroke.

4. When letters, taken out of context, resemble the letter *x*, it means that the writer has an obsession with death. Take the capital letters *H* and *S* out of context, and what do you see?

5. Sometimes a writer underlines a few words to emphasize a point. This writer underlines everything. I'd say that's a bit of overkill. Wouldn't you?

Who Was That Hitchhiker in Your Rearview Mirror?

The hitchhiker that you left in the dust was serial killer Aileen "Lee" Wuornos, the "Hitchhiker Hooker," whose life was the basis for the award-winning movie *Monster*. Wuornos confessed to the fatal shooting of seven men along the Florida highways.

Let's see how well your profile of Wuornos matches the reality of her life:

1. Her writing is too perfect.
   - **Profile:** Overly controlled writers are unpredictable. Everything may seem hunky-dory until one day, when something sets them off. Then watch out.
   - **Reality:** Between 1989 and 1991, Aileen Wuornos, who was bisexual, lived with her girlfriend, Tyria "Ty" Moore. During this two-year period, six of Wuornos's seven murders occurred when her relationship with Ty was on the rocks. Wuornos's bloodiest killing spree was triggered by a visit from Ty's sister. Wuornos feared that Ty would abandon her and return home to Ohio with her sister. During the three-week period, beginning with Tyria's sister's arrival, Wuornos murdered three men.

2. The vertical and horizontal loops of this writer's *I* are close to nonexistent.
   - **Profile:** The vertical loop represents the mother figure while the horizontal loop represents the father figure.
   - **Reality:** Aileen Wuornos's mother abandoned her when she was four years old. She never met her father, a convicted child molester who committed suicide in prison. She was raised by her alcoholic grandparents, who abused her physically, sexually, and emotionally.
3. The writer makes an extra wide left side margin.
   - **Profile:** Extra-wide left margins show that the writer wants to run away from the past.
   - **Reality:** Aileen Wuornos started selling her body at the age of eleven, was pregnant by fourteen, and by the age of fifteen had dropped out of school. After her grandmother died, Wuornos hit the road, where she became known as the "Hitchhiker Hooker."
4. Sometimes a writer underlines a few words to emphasize a point.
   - **Profile:** This writer underlines almost everything. That's a bit of overkill, don't you think? Excessive underliners also love to exaggerate.
   - **Reality:** Wuornos boasted that she had sex with 250,000 men, which is highly unlikely (equivalent to a rate of two men per hour each and every day for close to fifteen years). A propensity for underlining also indicates that the writer has a tendency to "overdo" it. Wuornos claimed that she shot her clients to defend herself against rape and torture. This may have been true in one instance. However, Wuornos shot all of her victims multiple times, usually in the back, chest, and head. She shot one man six times and another seven times.
5. When letters, taken out of context, resemble the letter *x*, it means that the writer has an obsession with death.
   - **Profile:** Out of context, the capital letters *H* and *S* resemble the letter *x*.

- **Reality:** Notice that Wuornos's signature also contains x's in the *A* in "Aileen" and the *s* in "Wuornos." From this writing it is no surprise that it was written while Wuornos was waiting on Death Row.

Take a look at one more interesting characteristic in Wuornos's writing: her lower loops, or more accurately, her squeezed lower loops. As you may recall from Chapter 2, lower loops correlate with a writer's sexual area. You might think that because Wuornos was a highly promiscuous prostitute, she would have a greatly exaggerated lower zone. But her lower loops are tight and narrow.

It's important to understand that lower loops show a person's sexual drive and appetite. Large, exaggerated lower loops show that a writer loves to think about and fantasize about sex, whereas small, shrunken loops indicate a person for whom sex is relatively unimportant. Even though Aileen Wuornos claimed to have had sex with more than a quarter million men, she may not have wanted or enjoyed sex at all. Ty Moore said of their relationship, "We were more like sisters than lovers."

Wuornos told the Florida Supreme Court: "I'm one who seriously hates human life and would kill again." The justices took her at her word, and upheld her death sentence. After she lost her appeal, Wuornos began fighting for a speedy execution. She said she wanted it "all to be over" as soon as possible. Wuornos was executed by lethal injection in October 2002. Aileen Wuornos was the tenth women to be put to death in the United States since the reinstatement of the death penalty in 1976. Her final words were: "I'll be back."

15

Mad Doctors

I will prescribe for the good of my patients according to my ability and my judgment and never do harm to anyone. To please no one will I prescribe a deadly drug, nor give advice which may cause his death.
From the Hippocratic Oath

When a doctor takes the Hippocratic Oath, he or she pledges to save lives, not take them, to heal and to help patients, not harm them. Statistically, very few doctors are serial killers; however, an unusually high percentage of serial killers are doctors. Why?

Whether they are killers who became doctors or doctors who became killers, mad doctors have certain advantages over other serial killers, including:

- Abundant opportunities to kill (easy access to vulnerable victims)
- The skills (their medical training) to take advantage of those opportunities
- The inherent power of their position (the respect and deference that is typically paid to physicians), which enables them to entrap victims and maintain their cover.

These advantages make it easier for doctors to murder and to get away with murder. This chapter is about three American "mad doctors" from three different eras who, between them, snuffed out well over one hundred innocent lives: Herman Webster Mudgett (late nineteenth century), Linda Burfield Hazzard (early twentieth century), and Michael Swango (late twentieth century).

Let's explore their methods and motivations, and identify the traits in their handwriting that might have warned us that their scripts were not ordinary doctor scribble, but prescriptions for murder.

Some have called Herman Webster Mudgett, MD, America's first serial killer. Mudgett was prolific. It is believed that he murdered well over a hundred people for fun and profit. There have been few serial killers as bold or as clever as Mudgett.

Linda Burfield Hazzard killed for money. It's believed that she starved at least forty of her patients to death. Even as they lay dying at Wilderness Heights, her Olalla, Washington sanitarium, she began collecting her booty. She found that a diamond ring came off an emaciated finger quite easily.

Mike Swango was a thrill killer. He got a rush out of putting people to sleep and watching them retch and shudder from the effects of the poisons and drugs he administered.

The Strange Case of Dr. Mudgett and Mr. Holmes

Chicago, 1893: Millions flocked to the shores of Lake Michigan to behold the great "White City" of the Chicago World's Fair. But beyond the glittering lights of the fair, on Chicago's South Side, Dr. Herman Webster Mudgett, a real-life "Jekyll and Hyde," was preparing for his next victim . . .

In 1896, ten years after Robert Louis Stevenson published *The Strange Case of Dr. Jekyll and Mr. Hyde*, a real-life doctor, Herman Webster Mudgett, confessed to the murder and torture of at least twenty-seven victims. Around the same time that Jack the Ripper was terrorizing London, Mudgett, using the name "H. H. Holmes," was beginning his career as a swindler, con artist, and serial killer.

As a teenager, Mudgett was fascinated with surgery. He would catch neighborhood cats and dogs and perform surgical "experiments" on them. A good student, Mudgett attended the University of Michigan Medical School in Ann Arbor, where he continued his experiments on human corpses he stole from the morgue. After graduating from medical school, he moved to Englewood, Illinois, a suburb of Chicago. There he began working as a pharmacist, calling himself Dr. Henry Howard Holmes. His employer, Mrs. Holton, was desperate for someone to help her run the drugstore since her pharmacist husband had taken ill. It wasn't long before Mrs. Holton mysteriously disappeared and "Dr. Holmes" took over the drugstore and began selling his own line of phony remedies. The business was highly profitable, and Mudgett quickly became a very rich man.

With his newfound wealth, Mudgett/Holmes built a 100-room hotel on Chicago's South Side. Holmes Castle, as the hotel came to be called, included a number of unique features specifically designed for the convenience of the evil doctor. Many of the rooms were soundproof and included secret peepholes. The sleeping chambers locked not from the inside but from the outside. Gas pipes and vents were connected to the rooms, with the controls in Mudgett's bedroom. There were also secret passages, false floors, and a torture chamber.

Mudgett would lure young women into his castle to spend the night. While they slept, he would pump lethal gas into their rooms, watching them die through his secret peepholes. Then he would open the false floors and slide his victims' corpses down chutes into his cellar. There, he would chop up their bodies and put the pieces in a vat of chemicals. Finally, he would sell their bleached skeletons to medical schools for a small fortune.

Imagine you're a young woman from the country visiting the 1893 Chicago World's Fair. You're enjoying a beautiful summer evening in a café overlooking the fairgrounds, which are illuminated by millions of electric lights. A boy in a crisp white uniform brings you a glass of sarsaparilla on a silver tray. He points to a

handsome gentleman seated across the way. On the tray is a handwritten note, inviting you to Holmes Castle.

Would there have been clues in his writing that might have
warned you of his evil intentions?

Here we have two samples of Dr. Mudgett's handwriting. At first
glance, these two signatures, both written by Mudgett, don't look
all that unusual. Recall that Ted Bundy's writing also looked "normal" to the untrained eye. Both Mudgett and Bundy were handsome, outwardly normal men who were skilled in gaining the
confidence of their victims. But if you look very closely at Mudgett's
writing, you'll see that there are a number of danger signs that
shout: "You can check into my castle . . . but you can't check out."

First, notice the blotch on the top of the *H* on his middle initial
in the "H. H. Holmes" signature and the puddle of ink on the *M*
in "Mudgett." Blotches, puddles, and muddy-looking writing
show murky and unclean thinking. These dark spots are signs
that he has obsessive, morbid fantasies and will indulge, uncontrollably, in his sensual and libidinal urges. It is interesting to note
that Jack the Ripper also had muddied handwriting.

The fact that the blotch on the top of his middle initial *H* resembles a dagger is no coincidence. Weapon-shaped structures in handwriting are always a bad sign. They indicate that the writer has
hostile impulses and will not hesitate to use violence. Weapon-
shaped structures show an especially dangerous person when they
are found in the personal pronoun "I" or in the signature. They also
often indicate a killer's weapon of choice. Mudgett, a trained doctor, used his surgeon's scalpel to dissect the corpses of his victims.

Also, notice how the ending stroke on the letter *s* in "Holmes" juts below the line. When an ending stroke of a middle-zone letter extends below the baseline, you are dealing with an aggressive and sneaky writer, who will use an underhanded and indirect approach to get what he wants. You can be sure that whatever a man like Mudgett might say, beneath the surface, he has a hidden agenda.

Blotched letters, weapon strokes, and ending strokes that jut below the base line all add up to one very bad man. As Mudgett himself wrote: "I was born with the devil in me. I could not help the fact that I was a murderer, no more than the poet can help the inspiration to sing . . . I was born with the 'Evil One' standing as my sponsor beside the bed where I was ushered into the world, and he has been with me ever since."

Herman Webster Mudgett was executed on May 7, 1896, nine days before his thirty-sixth birthday.

Erik Larson tells the remarkable story of Dr. Holmes, Mr. Mudgett, and the Chicago World's Fair in *The Devil in the White City: Murder, Magic and Madness at the Fair That Changed America.*

Dr. Hazzard's Starvation Diet

Claire Williamson turned to her sister. "Dora," she exclaimed, "I think I've found the answer!"

"It's right here," she said, referring to an advertisement for Dr. Linda Burfield Hazzard's book *Fasting for the Cure of Disease.* "An American doctor has an amazing new treatment that cures cancer, toothaches, psoriasis, heart trouble, stomach disturbances, tuberculosis, insanity, and female troubles."

The two wealthy British heiresses had been searching for relief from a variety of minor ills, including stomach and knee pain, headaches, and "female troubles." After corresponding with Dr. Hazzard and reading her book and brochure, they were excited about Dr. Hazzard's cure, and looked forward to taking a relaxing holiday at Dr. Hazzard's sanitarium for a few weeks.

On February 27, 1911, Dora and Claire Williamson entered Wilderness Heights, located in the small town of Olalla on the outskirts of Seattle. Dr. Hazzard was vivacious and charismatic.

She promised the sisters that she would rid them of the toxins that were causing imbalances in their bodies. At last! they thought.

Dr. Hazzard's treatment consisted of a strict regimen of water and a thin asparagus and tomato soup, along with daily enemas (of two to three hours) and vigorous massages to aid the body in shedding toxins.

At Wilderness Heights, there were many wealthy patrons. Like Claire and Dora, most were cared for in their own private cabins. The cabins had all the comforts of home—except food! I guess that's why the locals called the place Starvation Heights!

As the patients weakened and became bedridden, Dr. Hazzard would advise them to turn over their accounts, land deeds, and jewelry to her for safekeeping. Dr. Hazzard's husband Sam, a convicted bigamist and swindler, was the "closer." It was his job to persuade the weakest of patients to rewrite their wills, making his wife the sole beneficiary of their estates.

As her patients arrived and departed (to the other world), Hazzard became richer and richer.

Within a month, both Dora and Claire were emaciated, weak, and in agony. But Dr. Hazzard persuaded them that their pain was a good sign. It meant that they were eliminating the poisons from their bodies. Three months after the Williamsons' arrival at Wilderness Heights, Claire joined the list of "dearly departed" patients. She was only thirty-three. After Dr. Hazzard performed an autopsy, she filled out Claire's death certificate. Under "cause of death" Hazzard wrote "Cirrhosis of Liver."

Here is Dr. Hazzard's signature from Claire Williamson's death certificate. Do you see any red flags in her signature that might have warned prospective patients to spend their holidays elsewhere?

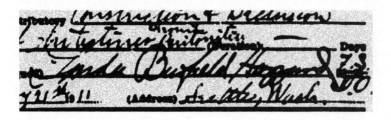

Remember the advice "Don't make connections with guys or gals whose handwriting slants in all directions" from Chapter 8? Do you see how the letters in Dr. Hazzard's signature slant in all directions? Some slant to the right, some slant to the left, while others are straight up and down? It appears that the doctor was moody and emotionally unstable.

Next, look at the *L* in "Linda." Do you see how it drops below the baseline? As we saw in Chapter 11, when letters sneak below the baseline, although the writer may appear to be aboveboard, below the surface trouble is brewing. While Hazzard pretended to be dedicated to healing, her true motive was stealing!

And do you see how the ending stroke of the *d* in "Hazzard" lurks below the baseline? I do believe that is the lurking lunatic stroke, a sign that the doctor was stealthy, sneaky, and secretive.

Perhaps the most telling red flag in Dr. Hazzard's writing is the most subtle. I want you to look very closely at the "Lin" in her first name. What do you see? Remember the "x" formation that Hitler placed in his name? Her letter *i* has become an *x*. This shows Hazzard's preoccupation with death.

After performing Claire Williamson's autopsy, Hazzard slid the rings off of Claire's bony fingers and placed them in her own jewelry box. Claire's elaborate gowns were hung neatly in the doctor's closet. Even the gold fillings from Claire's teeth were extracted and sold for money.

Claire's will, dated the day before she died, bequeathed her entire fortune to Linda Burfield Hazzard. Conveniently, Claire wrote of her decision to make her doctor the sole beneficiary of her estate on the last page of her diary.

The next step in the doctor's meticulous plan was to secure her investment in Dora Williamson. Hazzard declared to county officials that Dora was hopelessly insane and requested that she be granted guardianship of Dora. But Hazzard's plan was foiled by a determined patient. On July 22, 1911, aided by a sympathetic nurse and a relative, Dora managed to escape.

Dora went to the authorities to seek justice for her sister. Investigators learned that at least forty patients had died while under Hazzard's care. Interestingly, all of her "dearly departed" patients left all their money to her in their wills. Typically Dr. Hazzard would fill out her deceased patients' death certificates. Under "cause of death" she always scribed an assortment of maladies. However, on the occasion when a different doctor performed the autopsy, under "cause of death" the results were always the same: "starved to death."

On August 4, 1911, Linda Hazzard was charged with murder for intentionally starving Claire Williamson to death.

During Hazzard's trial, the defense claimed that "fasting specialist" Linda Hazzard was a healer and that many of her patients were already on their deathbeds when they entered the sanatorium. However, prosecution attorney Thomas Stevenson said that Hazzard wasn't a "fasting specialist" but a "financial starvationist." "A serpent who trod sly and stealthy, yet with all her craft left a trail of slime." Stevenson proved that Claire's will was forged and had been written by Dr. Hazzard. He also proved that the last entry in Claire's diary was not written by Claire, but was indeed also in the handwriting of Dr. Hazzard.

On February 4, 1912, Hazzard was found guilty of manslaughter and sentenced to twenty years of hard labor. She spent only two years in prison.

Eventually, she returned to Olalla and built a bigger and better sanitarium, as if nothing had ever happened.

Amazingly, Dr. Hazzard's books continue to sell. A number of Web sites promote the revised edition of Hazzard's *Fasting for the Cure of Disease,* touting its revolutionary technique as a way to "lose weight, increase energy, and reduce those middle-aged aches and pains."

Double-O-Swango: License to Kill

Mike Swango was different from the other medical students at Southern Illinois University. He was an ex-Marine and loner, who worked nights as an ambulance attendant, and seemed determined to spend as little time as possible doing the things medical students usually do, like studying, hanging out, and attending lectures and labs.

When he did attend class, he was in a world of his own, clumsy at dissection, ignorant of basic anatomy, and more than a little strange. If a professor chastised him for his ignorance, he would suddenly drop to the floor and do fifty pushups.

But what really got his classmates attention were Swango's interactions with patients. During rounds, Swango seemed aloof and disinterested. When patients passed away, he would write "DIED" on their charts in big red letters.

Like all medical students, Swango was assigned a number of patients to monitor. His classmates couldn't help but notice that an unusually high number of Swango's patients were dying suddenly and unexpectedly. It happened so often that they called him "Double-O-Swango," the doctor with the "license to kill."

Here's a Christmas card written by convicted killer Mike Swango, MD to a childhood friend. Can you find the red flags in Swango's handwriting?

You may use this gift with one condition : Do not destroy Bruce completely (leave a little for somebody else!). Merry Christmas, Gerry.

Mike

Here are some of the key traits and red flags that I found in Swango's script:

Puts up a facade

At first glance, Swango's writing looks fairly normal. It's neat and even—but there's something about it that should jog your memory. Do you recall the slow facade handwriting of Kenneth Bianchi? Extremely slow writing in a healthy adult is a red flag for danger. Like Bianchi, Swango took extra time to form each and every letter. His slow, carefully crafted handwriting shows that Swango creates a facade designed to keep his real motives hidden.

Looks out for number one

Notice how Swango made the G in "Gerry" look like the numeral 6. This trait is not necessarily a danger sign, but it is a sign that the writer is mathematically inclined. (I've noticed that accountants and meteorologists often have letters that resemble numbers in their handwriting.) Numbers are especially important to Dr. Swango.

Is controlled and detached

Swango's writing is fairly vertical, leaning neither to the left nor to the right. To write vertically takes a lot of control.

Vertical writers not only control their handwriting; they also control their emotions. They have learned to detach themselves from others and often work better with facts and objects than people.

Keeps his distance

Swango has abnormally wide spacing between his words. He even has abnormally wide spacing between individual letters. See the word "Christmas." The space between the C and the *h* has too much distance. Swango put a great deal of space between himself and others. His detachment prevented him from becoming close or intimate with people.

Is underhanded and devious

Did you notice the distorted communication letters in Swango's handwriting? Most people write their o's and a's in a counterclockwise direction. Look closely at Swango's o's and a's. Many are written backwards in a clockwise direction. When learning to write, children will often make backwards o's and a's; however, when you see them in an adult's handwriting, beware, because you are dealing with someone who is underhanded and devious.

During Swango's surgery rotation at Ohio State University, relatively healthy patients started dying under mysterious circumstances. While administrators were resistant to conducting an official investigation, unofficially they attributed these deaths to Swango's incompetence. After a year in the Ohio State University medical program, Swango was asked to leave.

He took a job as a paramedic in his hometown of Quincy, Illinois. At first, his coworkers in the ambulance corps thought Swango was strange but harmless. Some found his morbid sense of humor entertaining. That was to change one morning when Swango brought some donuts to work. Within an hour, four of his colleagues started experiencing severe stomach cramps, nausea, and dizziness. They continued to vomit for days. Swango, they later recalled, hadn't eaten any of the donuts. And come to think of it, he hadn't gotten sick, either.

After another incident, when two of his coworkers became ill after drinking soda, several members of the ambulance crew decided to check out Swango's locker while he was out on call. They discovered that Dr. Swango kept a box of ant poison in a duffle bag.

When investigators searched his house, in addition to more packages of ant poison, they found lots of numbers on carefully handwritten "homemade" recipes for a variety of poisons.

Mike Swango was convicted of six counts of aggravated battery and sentenced to five years in prison. He also lost his license to practice medicine. At his sentencing hearing, Judge Dennis Cashman told Swango: "It's clearly obvious to me that every man, woman and child in this community or anywhere else that you might go is in jeopardy as long as you are a free person . . . You deserve the maximum under the law because there is no excuse for what you have done."

But Swango was released after serving less than three years. Though banned from practicing medicine, Swango found it incredibly easy to find work using false identities and forged documents. The hospitals that hired him were impressed by both his credentials and his confident manner.

Living life on the edge, under assumed names, Swango rarely socialized. He had no friends. He trusted no one. But he did have several girlfriends. Outwardly, to his colleagues, Mike Swango appeared to be a perfectly normal guy.

While his girlfriends may have cared for him, Swango only pretended to be the loving, marrying kind. Behind the facade, Swango was unemotional and detached. In fact, he was so detached that he experimented on at least two girlfriends, poisoning them gradually, over time, so that he was able to observe the effects of the poison firsthand.

But every now and then, there would be a crack in his facade. The nurses he treated with indifference and arrogance were noticing certain things. That Mike Swango liked to work the night shift. That he often waited for them to leave a patient's room before entering. And that he liked to be alone with patients. But what they noticed most was that patients with good prognoses would suddenly die without warning on Dr. Swango's watch. Unfortunately, as James Stewart described in *Blind Eye: How the Medical Establishment Let a Doctor Get Away with Murder,* at hospital after hospital, when confronted with the evidence, doctors and hospital administrators gave Swango a free pass, enabling him to move on and kill again.

In 1994, Swango shifted his base of operations to Zimbabwe, Africa. In the remote Mnene Hospital, he assumed that the predominantly poor, uneducated patients would be easy prey. But in

Africa, where he least expected it, Swango was being watched very carefully.

Mnene's director, Dr. Christopher Zshiri, was wary of the American doctor. What were his motives? Why would a respected city doctor like him want to work in a small outpost hospital in Zimbabwe? But Swango seemed earnest and was a hard worker.

The hospital's Lutheran sisters told Zshiri that Swango was surly and rude. And they had suspicions that he was injecting patients with drugs. Some had died. But they had no evidence.

Until one night when patient Keneas Mzezewa awoke from a nap and saw blond, blue-eyed "Dr. Mike" standing over him. Swango smiled and stuck a large needle in Mzezewa's arm. Before Swango sauntered away he waved goodbye. Within minutes, Mzezewa could not move his arms or legs and could barely move his lips. Somehow, he managed to let out one piercing scream. The sisters rushed in and attempted to resuscitate him. Gradually, the paralysis went away. Terrified, Mzezewa told the sisters "Keep that bad man away." Sobbing, he continued, "Dr. Mike, he's no good! He tried to kill me."

When confronted, Swango adamantly denied giving anyone a shot. "He must have been hallucinating," he insisted. But a sister noticed that there was a syringe cap on the floor by the bed. It was true; the American doctor was murdering the patients of Mnene Hospital.

Swango was arrested and charged with murder. The government began its investigation of the deaths in Mnene. But before the trial, Michael Swango disappeared. He had escaped to Europe using another alias and false passport.

Eventually, the FBI was called in, and began putting together the pieces. They suspected that Michael Swango was a serial killer, responsible for killing as many as sixty people in the United States and Africa.

After hiding out in Europe for almost a year, Swango returned to the United States. When he disembarked at the Chicago airport, agents were waiting for him.

In his possession was a sheet of paper on which he had written down a passage from a book: "He could look at himself in a mirror and tell himself that he was one of the most powerful and dangerous men in the world. He could feel that he was a god in disguise." The passage was from *The Torture Doctor,* a biography of Herman Webster Mudgett.

On September 6, 2000, Swango was convicted for the murders of three patients at the Northport, New York, VA Medical Center. He is currently serving a life sentence, without the possibility of parole.

16

Busted by
a Handwriting Detective

From the forensic files, here are four real-life cases where hand-writing helped solve the crime. It's time to put on your thinking cap, Sherlock.

Case One: Murder, She Wrote

In the summer of 1991, 65-year-old Ghislaine Marchal, the wealthy widow of a French industrialist, was murdered in the basement of her grand villa on the Côte d'Azur. Lying in a pool of blood on her boiler room floor, Mme. Marchal had been bludg-eoned on the head with a block of wood and stabbed more than a dozen times. On the inside of the boiler room door was a bloody handprint and the words "OMAR M'A TUER" (French for "Omar killed me") written in blood.

Omar Raddad, Mme. Marchal's Moroccan gardener, was missing, and so was four thousand francs.

In court, a blood expert testified that the words on the door were written in the victim's own blood. Two handwriting experts testified that the handwriting on the door was consistent with a sample of the victim's writing from a crossword puzzle.

In 1994, based almost entirely on the message written on the boiler room door, 34-year-old Omar Raddad was convicted and sentenced to eighteen years in prison.

A photo of the writing on the door is shown below.

What do you think? In her last dying moments, did Ghislaine Marchal dip her finger in her own blood and write the message on the door? Did she solve her own murder?

Case Two:
Bird Dog's Life Is in Your Hands

An attorney is in the middle of a criminal trial. His client, affectionately known as "Bird Dog," has been accused of a double homicide. Bird Dog insists that he is innocent. An anonymous note has recently been found in a prison library. In the note, the writer brags about killing the very same two victims that Bird Dog is accused of killing. There are details in the note that only the true killer would know.

The attorney believes this note proves his client is innocent. But who is Podge, the name signed at the bottom of the note?

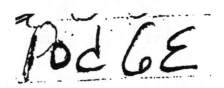

Case Three:
Ralph Kosloski, Bank Robber?

Ralph Kosloski went into a bank with a note that read. "I have a gun. Please hand over All $50 and $20 Put in bag." Standing in line behind Ralph was a newspaper reporter. The reporter happened to glance at the note that Ralph was holding. The reporter quickly stepped outside the bank and called the police. As Ralph was handing the bank teller the note, the police nabbed him and hauled his ass down to jail.

Ralph lives in a group home. When he didn't return to the home, the social workers panicked. Local television showed Ralph's photo on the news with the words "Man Missing." A police officer saw his picture and contacted his social workers. When the officer informed them that Ralph was in jail for bank robbery, they were shocked. They told the police that Ralph had the mental capacity of a six year old. Bail was set and Ralph returned to the group home.

Ralph claimed that while he was panhandling downtown, a man had come up to him and said, "See that pretty blonde bank teller? She's my wife. Give her this note." Ralph said that he simply went into the bank and gave the note to the lady behind the counter.

Is Ralph telling the truth? Could Ralph Kosloski have written the bank robbery note? Here's a copy of the actual bank note:

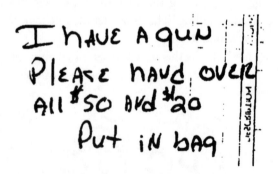

Here's a sample of Ralph Kosloski's handwriting:

I HAVE A ſ°ſ OVER
PEEL', ſſſ
ALL. ſc.ſ.ſ.
ſſ,ſo
P.ſ.ſ. ſ. ſ Aſ

Case Four:
Der Stern, *der Diary, und der Missing Millions*

Gerd Heidemann, an investigative reporter for *Der Stern* magazine, told his editors, "In April 1945, a plane went down near Dresden. It crashed and burned. These documents only survived because they were sealed in a metal-lined container."

"But where have they been all these years?" asked his editor.

"They were in the safekeeping of a farmer living in Boernersdorf."

Then Heidemann showed his editors his incredible discovery: the secret, handwritten diary of Adolf Hitler.

Top handwriting experts including Max Frei-Sulzer, former head of the Zurich police forensic science department, and Ordway Hilton, a document specialist from the United States, were called in to verify the authenticity of the diary. They were asked to compare pages of the diary to samples of Hitler's handwriting taken from the German Federal Archives. They confirmed that the diary matched the writing samples they had of Hitler.

Stern paid 9.9 million marks (approximately $5 million) for the 62 handwritten volumes of the diary. On April 25, 1983, the magazine published the first installment, which created a sensation. Newspapers and magazines all over the world lined up to buy reprint rights from *Stern*.

Meanwhile, the West German police and a team of forensic experts tested the paper and ink of the diary. Ultraviolet light revealed that the paper contained a whitening agent that had first been used in 1954. Each volume was wrapped with a black ribbon and sealed. An analysis of the ribbons showed that they contained polyester and viscose, materials that were developed after the war. A test on the evaporation of chloride from the ink revealed that the text had been written less than a year before.

The handwriting experts were right. The government's forensic experts were also right. How could that be?

Solution to Case One:
Murder, She Wrote

A while back, when I was doing research for this book, I read about the case of Mme. Ghislaine Marchal in David Owen's *Hidden Evidence: Forty True Crimes and How Forensic Science Helped Solve Them*. Here was a case in which the victim solved her own murder. It all sounded so reasonable. In her last dying moments, the wounded victim writes the name of her attacker in her own blood. Case closed.

But when I saw the photograph of the victim's writing on the boiler room door, my first thought was: "Something is definitely wrong here." And then I realized they had convicted the wrong man.

Notice how clearly "Omar m'a tuer" is written. The letters are basically well-formed, in alignment, and easy to read. A woman who was just hit on the head, stabbed at least 12 times, and is bleeding to death would not have the steadiest of hands.

I've looked at many wills written by people at death's door. Their writing is weak and erratic, for it is difficult (if not impossible) to write firmly and neatly when you're feeling sick and tired, or in terrible pain, or drowsy from medication.

Also, notice that the bloody message was written above the door handle, well over three feet off the ground. How could a person who's been bashed in the head and stabbed again and again write such a note? The bloody writing is not smeared or dripping down the door. The writing is rather crisp, steady, and legible. Did Mme. Marchal stand up, dip her finger in her wounds, and write those words above the door handle? The police found her body lying face down on the floor. If she were to write a note, wouldn't she have scribbled something on the floor or on the lower part of a wall or door?

It just didn't add up. I was convinced that Omar was framed. The French government had accused and prosecuted an innocent man based on a misinterpretation of handwriting evidence. After a few hours of Googling, I learned that many more things about this case didn't add up. DNA testing of the "Omar m'a tuer" message and a bloody handprint left on the door revealed that the blood was a mixture of Marchal's blood and the blood of a man. But that man was not Omar Raddad. A forensic expert testified that the murder had actually been committed one day earlier, when Raddad had been visiting friends and relatives in another town. Two different handwriting experts found inconsistencies between the letters written in blood and those in the crossword puzzle.

Had the first investigators, prosecutors, and handwriting experts used common sense, they would have known immediately that the victim couldn't have possibly written those words on the door.

Who framed Omar Raddad? It's likely that if police find the

person who did write the bloody accusation, they will have the real murderer. In fact, French police have refocused their investigation on two other men: Christian Veilleux, Marchal's estranged son, who inherited a fortune upon her death, and the cleaning lady's beau, a man nicknamed "Pierrot the insane one." Neither man has been arrested or charged with the crime.

After serving over seven years in prison, Omar was granted "partial amnesty" by French President Jacques Chirac in 1998 and released from prison, but he has never been officially cleared. Omar is currently working as a butcher in Marseilles, and is still trying to clear his name.

Solution to Case Two: Bird Dog's Life Is in Your Hands

There are more than a thousand prisoners in the county jail. If you had time, and a court order, you could try to get handwriting samples from every possible suspect and compare them to the "Podge" note.

Sometimes, trying to find the writer of an anonymous letter is like searching for a needle in a haystack. I've had many cases where I've had to sift through the handwriting of hundreds of suspects. For instance, there was the case of Laurie H. and the threatening letters. Laurie, an employee in a large company, found a series of anonymous death threats in her locker. She reported them to her boss, who reported them to the head of security, who hired me to find out who was writing the letters. After comparing the letters to the handwriting of more than 600 employees, I found a match. The person who was writing the threatening letters to Laurie was, in fact, Laurie herself! Apparently, she had been planning to sue her employer for promoting a "hostile work environment."

The case of the mysterious Podge was far less complicated. I looked at the Podge letter for a few minutes. I told Bird Dog's attorney: "The man who wrote this note is in cell block 6E."

"How do you know that?" he asked.

"It says so right here," I replied.

"Huh?" he responded.

"This doesn't say 'Podge.' It says 'Pod 6E.' He was telling someone to contact him in Pod 6E." (A "pod" is a type of prison cell block.)

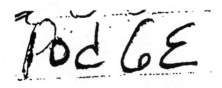

Solution to Case Three:
Ralph Kosloski, Bank Robber?

One of the most difficult tasks for a handwriting expert is to positively eliminate a suspect. How can you prove that someone didn't write a note? You might see dozens of a suspects' handwritten letters. You may have that suspect sit down in front of you and fill up an entire notebook with samples of his writing. But how do you know that he doesn't have another style of handwriting? How can you be sure that the suspect sitting in front of you isn't faking it?

The public defender's office hired me to answer this question: Could that bank robbery note have been written by Ralph Kosloski?

I met Ralph in his group home. He was sweet, childlike, and scared to death. I sat next to him and asked him to write "I have a gun." At that request, Ralph started to cry, "But I don't have a gun. I don't have a gun."

"I know," I reassured him, "but write it anyhow."

Ralph struggled painfully through my dictations.

By the time I was done, I knew that Ralph was innocent. How?

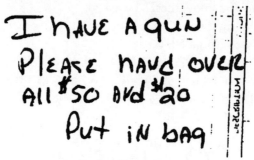

Bank robbery note

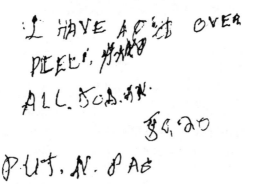

Ralph Kosloski's handwriting

Just as a six year old cannot skillfully imitate the handwriting of an adult, an unskilled writer cannot write above his capabilities. The bank robbery note was written quickly, by someone with a high degree of skill and motor control. After talking with his social workers, his doctor, and a psychiatrist, and after observing him firsthand, I knew that Ralph Kosloski wasn't faking it. He truly did not have the skill or motor control to write that note. He was telling the truth. The District Attorney's office agreed, and dropped all charges against Ralph Kosloski.

Solution to Case Four:
Der Stern, *der Diary, und der Missing Millions*

Stern's team of handwriting experts was certain that that the handwriting in the diary matched the handwriting in the Hitler archives. The government's team of police and forensic experts was convinced that the diary was not a World War II artifact, but had been written nearly forty years later.

They were both right. How could that be?

The handwriting in the diary did indeed match the samples from the official archives. It's just that those samples weren't actually written by Hitler.

A petty con artist and art forger named Konrad Kujau had not only forged the diary, he had also managed to forge the samples in the archives!

Here is Kujau's fake Hitler signature and his own (genuine) signature:

Kujau was sentenced to four and a half years in prison for fraud. After his release, he parlayed his notoriety into a successful—and honest—career as an expert art forger, selling his certified, hand-painted forgeries of famous paintings.

PART IV

Whodunits

⤆

17

Profile of an Axe Murderer

Lizzie Borden took an axe
And gave her mother forty whacks.
When she saw what she had done
She gave her father forty-one.

Or did she?

On August 4, 1892, in the small town of Fall River, Massachu-setts, an "unidentified subject" (UNSUB) crept into an upstairs bedroom of the Borden house. The UNSUB took a hatchet and whacked Abby Borden nineteen times in the face and head. Ninety minutes later, Andrew Borden was dealt ten whacks to his face while he napped on the sofa. Contrary to the famous rhyme, the real total was no more than twenty-nine.

Andrew Jackson Borden, seventy years of age, lived with his second wife, Abby, sixty-four, and his two unmarried adult daughters by his late first wife. Emma Lenora, the elder, was forty-one and Lizzie Andrew was thirty-two.

Andrew Borden was one of the wealthiest businessmen in Fall River, yet he chose to live with his family in a small house in an unfashionable part of town. Their simple house had no electric-ity or indoor plumbing—luxuries enjoyed by those with far less money than Andrew Borden. His daughters felt that his frugal nature was ruining their chances for social success.

The Borden household, never known as a cheery place, had been particularly gloomy Wednesday, the day before the brutal murders. Emma was visiting friends in Fairhaven, about fifteen miles away. Andrew, Abby, and Bridget, the family's housekeeper, had all been feeling poorly, complaining of terrible stomach pains and nausea. Bridget felt that the mutton stew that they had been eating for the last several days was the reason behind their suffering. She begged Mr. Borden to let her throw it out, but his thrifty nature would allow no such thing.

On Thursday morning, Andrew left for work at around 9:00 AM. A few minutes later, Abby instructed Bridget to wash all the windows. Andrew returned from work at 10:40 AM, said he was feeling sick, and went into the parlor to rest. Bridget, also ill, went upstairs to take a nap.

As the town clock struck 11:00 AM, Bridget heard Lizzie call, "Come down quick! Father's dead! Somebody came in and killed him!"

There were no signs of forced entry. The doors were locked and there was no evidence of anything being stolen. That made Bridget and Lizzie—the only people in the house other than Abby and Andrew Borden—the prime suspects.

Bridget told police that she had been washing windows most of the morning and went up to her room to lie down. Her story never wavered. But Lizzie's story had holes and inconsistencies. Police found human blood on a petticoat and on the sole of her shoe. When questioned about it, she said that it was from a "flea bite," a euphemism for menstrual blood. Nearly a year later, Lizzie Borden was tried for the murder of her father and stepmother. In what was called "the trial of the century," Lizzie was defended by the best legal team her father's money could buy.

Overwhelming evidence placed Lizzie at the time and scene of the murders. The prosecutors showed that Lizzie detested her stepmother and feared that her father's money would go to her stepmother's family. One witness testified that she saw Lizzie burn a dress shortly after the murders. Yet it took the jury of all white males just sixty-eight minutes to declare her not guilty. Jurors evidently could not believe that a demure, well-mannered, church-going former Sunday school teacher was capable of whacking her parents to death. Her handwriting, however, tells another story:

First, notice that Lizzie's writing lacks spontaneity. It appears stiff, with a rigid and repetitive pattern. Compare Lizzie's writing to Kenneth Bianchi's and Mike Swango's. All have the same monotonous, artificial quality. Like the writing of Bianchi (who was seen as the perfect boyfriend, father, and employee, until he was unmasked as the Hillside Strangler) and of Swango (the obsessive poisoner who posed as a healer), Lizzie's stylized, slowly drawn writing shows how she was able to conceal her true self and motives behind a facade.

Often, people with this sort of stiff and mechanical-looking writing show little emotion. This was true of Mike Swango, who matter-of-factly told families inquiring about a loved one, "He died."

One of the police officers described Lizzie's demeanor less than two hours after the bodies were discovered:

Lizzie stood by the foot of the bed, and talked in the most calm and collected manner; her whole bearing was most remarkable under the circumstances. There was not the least indication of agitation, no sign of sorrow or grief, no lamentation of the heart, no comment on the horror of the crime, and no expression of a wish that the criminal be caught. All this, and something that, to me, is indescribable,

*gave birth to a thought that was most revolting. I thought,
at least, she knew more than she wished to tell.*

Recall that the day before the murders, Andrew, Abby, and Bridget had all been feeling poorly, which Bridget attributed to the mutton stew. In fact, a clerk at Smith's Drug Store stated that the day before the murders, Lizzie had tried to purchase ten cents' worth of prussic acid (hydrogen cyanide in solution), which Lizzie claimed she needed to kill insects. When the clerk refused to sell it to her without a prescription, Lizzie became agitated, and told him that she had had no trouble purchasing it there before. Another witness said that Lizzie had tried to buy the same poison from a different drugstore earlier that week.

Stiff, artificial facade writing is also typical of poisoners. Perhaps it has to do with the deceptive, stealthy nature of the poisoner's crime. It's no coincidence that Graham Young, the Teacup Poisoner(A), Mike Swango (B), and Lizzie Borden (C) were all facade writers:

A

B

C

In Lizzie's case, hacking her father and stepmother to death with an axe may not have been her original plan, but became necessary after the poison failed to have the predicted effect.

Though Lizzie's first choice of lethal weapon may have been poison, her handwriting shows that she would not hesitate to use other deadly weapons. Do you see the noose-like stroke on the bottom of Lizzie's *M*'s and the distorted hook on the *B* in "Borden"? And could that strange, squared-off formation on the *M* in "Mr" be the start of an axe?

Look at the way Lizzie wrote her capital *S*. Do you see how it ends with a final stroke that curves high and upward? Flamboyant ending strokes show a writer who likes to be noticed. So, while Lizzie's basic demeanor was stilted and unemotional, there was another side of her that enjoyed extravagant gestures and attention-getting behavior. She demonstrated this showy side in court, where, according to observers, her elaborate fainting scenes helped her win over the jury.

Finally, notice how the final stroke of Lizzie's *M* in the words "Mr." and "Miss" forms a loop that sneaks into the lower zone, breaks, and then rises back up to form an X. Could this unusual formation in Lizzie's lower zone be a sign of hidden, possibly taboo, feelings about sex?

Five weeks after she was acquitted, Lizzie and her sister moved into a mansion in Fall River's most fashionable neighborhood. A few years later, a glamorous actress named Nance O'Neil, rumored to be Lizzie's lover, moved into the house and Emma moved out. Lizzie and Emma never saw one another again. Lizzie died in Fall River on June 1, 1927, at the age of sixty-six. Emma died nine days later in Newmarket, New Hampshire.

18

⮌

Who Wrote
the JonBenét Ramsey
Ransom Note?

5:51 AM *December 26, 1996*

"Help me Jesus, help me," the woman cried to the 911 operator. As the woman fumbled to hang up the phone the faint voice of a boy was heard in the background followed by the voice of a grown man who grumbled, "We weren't speaking to you." To that, the young voice muttered, "But what did you find?"

The Ramsey House,
755 15th Street

Boulder, Colorado—Police arrived at the Ramsey house within seven minutes of the 911 call. Patsy Ramsey told detective Linda Arndt that she had risen early on that cold December morning. She had gone downstairs at 5:45 to make some coffee and, as she did every morning, she took the back spiral staircase to the kitchen. At the bottom of the stairs, she found this three-page note:

Mr. Ramsey,

Listen carefully! We are a group of individuals that represent a small foreign faction. We do respect your bussiness but not the country that it serves. At this time we have your daughter in our posession. She is safe and unharmed and if you want her to see 1997, you must follow our instructions to the letter.

You will withdraw $118,000.00 from your account $100,000 will be in $100 bills and the remaining $18,000 in $20 bills. Make sure that you bring an adequate size attache to the bank. When you get home you will put the money in a brown paper bag. I will call you between 8 and 10 am tomorrow to instruct you on delivery. The delivery will be exhausting so I advise you to be rested. If we monitor you getting the money early, we might call you early to arrange an earlier delivery of the

money and hence d earlier
~~delivery~~ pick-up of your daughter.
Any deviation of my instructions
will result in the immediate
execution of your daughter. You
will also be denied her remains
for proper burial. The two
gentlemen watching over your daughter
do not particularly like you so I
advise you not to provoke them.
Speaking to anyone about your
situation, such as Police, F.B.I., etc.,
will result in your daughter being
beheaded. If we catch you talking
to a stray dog, she dies. If you
alert bank authorities, she dies.
If the money is in any way
marked or tampered with, she
dies. You will be scanned for
electronic devices and if any are
found, she dies. You can try to
deceive us but be warned that
we are familiar with Law enforcement
countermeasures and tactics. You
stand a 99% chance of killing
your daughter if you try to out
smart us. Follow our instructions

and you stand a 100% chance
of getting her back. You and
your family are under constant
scrutiny as well as the authorities.
Don't try to grow a brain
John. You are not the only
fat cat around so don't think
that killing will be difficult
Don't underestimate us John.
Use that good southern common
sense of yours. It is up to
you now John!

                        Victory!

                        S.B.T.C

After reading the note, Patsy stated that she yelled for her husband, John. When they looked in their little girl's room, she was missing.

John Ramsey contacted his bank to make arrangements to pick up the requested $118,000.

The note said that the kidnappers would call between 8 and 10 AM. But 10:00 AM came and went with no phone call. By midafternoon, Detective Arndt suggested that John Ramsey and his friends Fleet White and John Fernie search the house for "anything unusual."

They started in the basement. Within minutes, White yelled "Call an ambulance."

John Ramsey ran up the basement stairs carrying a young girl in his arms. The girl's arms were raised above her head. There was a white cloth wrapped around the girl's neck and a matching white string hung from her right wrist. John Ramsey placed the girl on the marble floor of the front foyer. Her lips were blue. The 6-year-old beauty queen had been brutally murdered.

For years, experts and non-experts have been debating about what really happened in the Ramsey house in the early hours of December 26. The investigators, speculators, and prognosticators have generally been divided into two camps. One side has argued that JonBenét was murdered by an intruder who crept into the house and killed her in a botched kidnapping attempt. The other side maintains that JonBenét was almost certainly killed by a family member.

Will we ever know the truth? Maybe not. But one thing is clear. The ransom note found on the back staircase is one of the most important pieces of evidence in this case. Whoever wrote the note holds the secret to who killed JonBenét Ramsey.

The War and Peace of Ransom Notes

The Ramsey ransom note is unique in several respects. At 370 words, it's extremely long. Whether they are handwritten, typed, or composed of cutouts from magazines, most ransom notes are short and to the point (fewer words mean less evidence), and go something like this:

> "Have daughter. She is safe. Want $850,000, small bills, don't call police—or she dies. Will contact you."

Could the "ransom note" be a sham, not a genuine kidnapping note? The length of the note is the first red flag.

Ransom notes are usually thought out and written prior to the crime. However, the writer of this particular ransom note wrote it in the victim's house. In fact, the paper was taken from a legal pad found in the home. The writer flipped through the pad, wrote a "practice" note on sheet twenty-five, discarded that note, started another note on sheet twenty-six, discarded that note, and finally composed the three-page note shown above.

The pen used to write the note was a felt-tip Sharpie that the Ramseys kept in a container on the kitchen counter.

A Kidnapping Gone Wrong . . . or an Accident or Murder Made to Look Like a Kidnapping?

The slowly drawn look of the writing, the wavering lines, and the crude lettering in the ransom note indicate that the writer was trying to conceal his or her identity, most likely by writing with his or her nondominant hand. To fully understand how long it would take to write this note, try disguising your printing by writing a three-page letter with your nondominant hand.

It appears that the writer was not overly concerned with being discovered. This would suggest that he or she may have been in the house before and felt comfortable there.

Would an intruder who wanted to extort money by kidnapping a little girl break into a house, search for a pen and paper, sit in a lit room (you can't write a three-page letter in the dark), and take the time to write two or more drafts of a three-page letter in a disguised handwriting?

The writer placed the note on the back stairway. Did the writer know that Patsy Ramsey always took the back staircase in the morning? The note contained detailed information of the Ramseys' finances, demanding $118,000 in cash, the amount John Ramsey had recently received as a bonus. (The bonus was actually $118,117.50.) And the writer knew that the Boulder businessman was a southerner (Ramsey was originally from Atlanta), writing, "Use that good southern common sense of yours."

Whoever wrote the note most likely knew intimate details about John Ramsey's life and may have been familiar with and comfortable in the Ramsey house.

~~Mispelling~~ . . . ~~Misspeling~~ . . . ~~mizspelling~~ Misspelling

I find that when a person writes a letter he or she concentrates the most in the first few sentences. After a few paragraphs, however, the hand (and the brain) relax and a more natural language and script emerge.

The writer of the ransom note starts off trying to give us the impression that he or she is uneducated by misspelling the words "bussiness" and "posession." However, by the second paragraph the writer is using sophisticated words such as "attaché" and "monitor." And there are no more misspellings.

The letter begins with "Mr. Ramsey," addressing Mr. Ramsey formally, as one would address a stranger. But by the final paragraph, the writer calls him "John." This suggests that the writer may have had a familiar or even intimate relationship with John Ramsey.

In the first paragraph, the writer uses "group," "we," and "our," but, by the second and third paragraphs, the writer switches between "I," "my," and "our." This letter was not written by "a group," as stated in the first paragraph, but by an individual working alone or, perhaps, with input from a collaborator.

More Clues

Let's see what else we can tell about the writer from his or her handwriting. I've numbered each line of the last paragraph of the note for easy reference.

- Line #1: The letter *d* in "and" ends with a checkmark-like tick stroke which shows us that the writer was frustrated and angry. But by subconsciously adding the tick mark to the *d* the writer formed a letter that resembles a symbol—a musical note. This tells us that the writer likes music.
- Notice that the *g*'s (lines #2, #5, #8, and #10) have incomplete loops, a sign that the writer's sex life is incomplete or unfulfilled.
- Line #3: Do you see how the *y* in the word "your" thickens at the bottom, forming a club stroke? When tempers flare, this writer can be cruel and brutal.
- Line #2: Notice how the *g* in the word "getting" in line #2 crosses into the word "family," making an *x* formation. Remember, *x* structures where they don't belong show that the writer is thinking about death. The fact that the *x* occurs through the word "family" is significant.
- Line #5: Do you see anything unusual about the word "a" (the word before the word "brain")? It resembles a phallus, a sign that this writer has bizarre sexual habits.
- Finally, notice that most of the lowercase *a*'s in this note have a little "hood," similar to the hood on a typewritten *a*? Hooded *a*'s are more likely to occur in the writing of a female.

The Scene of the Crime

Three family members were in the house on the night JonBenét Ramsey was killed:

1. Burke Ramsey: Older brother of JonBenét. Burke was almost ten at the time of his sister's death. Thirteeen

days after JonBenét was killed, Burke reportedly told a child psychologist that he was "getting on with my life."
2. John Ramsey: Father of JonBenét. John helped build Access Graphics into a billion-dollar computer firm. John discovered JonBenét's body in the cellar of his fifteen-room mansion.
3. Patricia Ramsey: Mother of JonBenét. Patsy, as Miss West Virginia, competed in the 1977 Miss America pageant.

Handwriting samples were taken from hundreds of individuals including John, Patsy, and Burke Ramsey. The Colorado Bureau of Investigation's handwriting expert, Chet Ubowski, determined that neither John Ramsey nor Burke Ramsey wrote the ransom note. However, Patsy Ramsey could not be ruled out. The Ramseys have adamantly maintained that the crime was committed by an intruder.

Patsy or No Patsy

Based on the language and handwriting traits in the note, we have a profile that identifies a number of likely characteristics in the writer's background, knowledge, and personality. It's reasonable to assume that Patsy Ramsey would know intimate details about John Ramsey, and of course, she would feel comfortable calling him John. She would feel at home in the Ramsey house. She would know where the pen and paper were kept. She's tidy and neat and would probably automatically put the pen and paper back where they belong. She's educated. She would be familiar with the back stairway, which she used to go down to the kitchen in the mornings. And she's musical. As for her sexual habits, temper, and thoughts about death and her family, I wouldn't dare to speculate. So Patsy Ramsey fits certain characteristics in our profile. But how does her handwriting compare to the handwriting in the ransom note?

The two most important factors in identifying the writer of an anonymous letter are: matching patterns and overwhelming odds. The more patterns and characteristics in the anonymous writing that match the writing of the suspect, the more overwhelming are the odds that you've found your anonymous writer.

Consider this scenario: Someone has just robbed the bank on Main Street. The robbery has been captured on video tape. You can tell that the robber is over six feet tall and is Caucasian. However, since he (or she) was wearing sunglasses, a heavy overcoat, hat, gloves, a fake beard, and possibly a false nose, you don't have much to go on.

But let's say the teller was very observant, and noticed that the robber had an Adam's apple, so obviously the robber was a male, and he was missing two front teeth. That helps to narrow your field of possible suspects, but not much. But let's say the teller remembers that the robber had a long scar on his neck below his left ear and that when he took his hand out of his pocket, she could see he had a red and black spider tattoo on his wrist with the date 1954 in Gothic characters above the spider. There's a pretty good chance that if you find a man who matches all of these characteristics, and there's nothing that absolutely rules him out—like a rock-solid alibi—you've found your bank robber.

So just because a suspect is tall and white, doesn't mean he robbed the bank on Main Street. And just because one or two features of a suspect's known handwriting match the anonymous writing doesn't mean you've caught your man (or your woman). But as you find more and more features in the anonymous writing that correspond to the known script of a suspect, the greater the odds are that your suspect is the anonymous writer. This is especially true if the matching features or characteristics in the known and anonymous writing are odd or unique.

Some anonymous letter writers print their letters instead of using cursive, thinking that printing will be impossible to identify. Generally, cursive writing is more distinctive than printing, especially "block" capital letters like those in the letters containing anthrax that were mailed to various individuals in 2001. But the printing in the Ramsey ransom note is quite distinctive, with many unique letter forms. Partly, this is because the writer combined capital and lower-case letters.

Let's look at some of the unique letter formations that appear in Patsy Ramsey's handwriting and the ransom note. Patsy Ramsey's known handwriting samples in the following graphics are from multiple sources, including exemplars she provided to the Boulder District Attorney.

Compare Patsy Ramsey's *abc*'s with the letter formations from the ransom note:

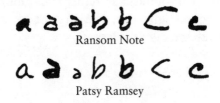

Ransom Note

Patsy Ramsey

Some of the more unique features that you might want to observe in both the ransom note and Patsy's writing are:

1. Both writers use a copybook *a*.
2. Both writers make an angular typewriter-like *a* made with two hand movements.
3. Both writers make a curved typewriter-like *a* made in one hand movement.

Compare these three very unique *d*'s in the ransom note (top) to those in Patsy Ramsey's writing (bottom):

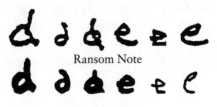

Ransom Note

Patsy Ramsey

There are three variations of the lower case *d* in both the ransom note and Patsy's writing:

1. In the first *d,* the stem bends inward to the left in the middle and is made in two hand movements.
2. The second *d* is made in one hand movement with the stem of the *d* curving outward to the right.
3. The circular portion of the third *d* does not end at the bottom of the stem. Instead it ends one quarter of the way up from the bottom. Also, the stem crosses inside the circular part of the letter rather than running tangentially along the right edge. The curve of the stem is very similar to the stem of the first *d*.

Look carefully at these *f*'s and *g*'s:

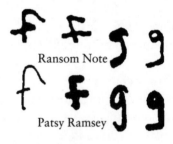

Both the ransom note writer (top) and Patsy Ramsey (bottom) have a curved *f* and an angular, boxy *f*.

There are at least two variations of lower-case *g*'s in the ransom note (top). One has a little hood in the top right corner, where the writer started the letter. The other "g" has a very distinctive, squared-off lower extension. Neither *g* has a completed lower loop.

Patsy Ramsey's *g*'s (bottom) share these very same characteristics.

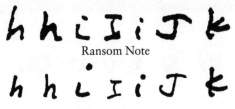

Ransom Note

Patsy Ramsey

Notice the unique curves and angles. Both writers have *L*-shaped *i*'s and cupped *i*'s. Both place their *i* dots in the same relative position as they move left to right. And both make their personal pronoun "I"'s with curved stems and angled horizontal strokes that point in the same directions.

Both writers make very unusual *n*'s that look like inverted *v*'s. And notice how both writers make *p*'s that are oval shaped and that are square.

Ransom Note

Patsy Ramsey

The *q*'s resemble the number 8 in both scripts, while some of the *s*'s resemble a reversed number 2:

Ransom Note

Patsy Ramsey

Look at the beginnings and endings of these *u*'s, *v*'s, *y*'s, and *z*'s:

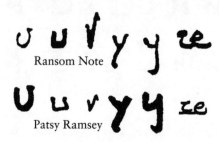

Ransom Note

Patsy Ramsey

Anonymous letter writers who try to disguise their writing often give themselves away by subconsciously falling into their everyday patterns. This can be seen not only in how they form individual letters—in their unique angles, overhangs, curves, and stroke endings—but also in how letters within words relate to one another.

For example, notice how both the ransom note writer and Patsy Ramsey connect their *t*'s in "getting." The first *t*-bar extends to the stem of the second *t* but not beyond. And the *t*-bar on the second *t* is noticeably lower than the *t*-bar on the first *t*.

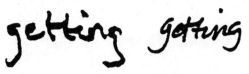

Ransom Note   Patsy Ramsey

Both writers similary connect the *f* to the following *o* in the word "foreign":

Ransom Note   Patsy Ramsey

Both writers connect letters in the same way in the words "so," "to," and "two":

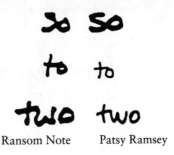

Ransom Note   Patsy Ramsey

Look at the *th* connections in the words "think," "southern," and "with":

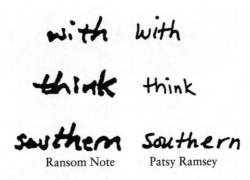

Ransom Note   Patsy Ramsey

See how the *c* connects to the bottom of the *o* in "constant":

Ransom Note   Patsy Ramsey

In both "brains," the *r* touches the *a*:

brain brain

Ransom Note   Patsy Ramsey

Look at the *t* and *o* connections in "monitor":

monitor   minitor
Ransom Note   Patsy Ramsey

Scrutinize the *tru* connections in the words "instructions," "instruction," and "instruct":

instructions   instruction

instruct   instruct
Ransom Note   Patsy Ramsey

Notice how the *tu* and the *ti* connect in the word "situation":

situation   situation
Ransom Note   Patsy Ramsey

Observe the similarities in the *en* in "sense":

sense   sense
Ransom Note   Patsy Ramsey

Compare the way both writers connect the letters in the word "your." The *y* and *o* are pressed closely together. The *o* and the *u* are connected by a thread. And both writers leave space between the letters *u* and *r*.

Ransom Note   Patsy Ramsey

In the word "pick," the *c* and *k* are joined at the bottom:

Ransom Note   Patsy Ramsey

In the word "electronic," both writers connect the same two sequences of letters: *el* and *ctro*.

Ransom Note   Patsy Ramsey

Some writers are in the habit of frequently making one letter higher or lower than others. Notice how each writer makes the *s* higher than the surrounding letters in "respect":

Ransom Note   Patsy Ramsey

Often overlooked in comparisons of anonymous and known handwriting are punctuation marks and their frequency and position.

The thick comma in the "$100,000" from the ransom note ends with a sharp lower point that curves to the right. The comma that Patsy wrote after "1997" ends the same way.

$ 100,000   1997,

Ransom Note   Patsy Ramsey

Could so many similarities be a coincidence?

The Twist

On August 16, 2006, almost ten years after JonBenét's body was discovered in the basement of her home, and two months after Patsy Ramsey lost her battle with ovarian cancer, an American teacher, John Mark Karr, was detained by authorities in Bangkok, Thailand. On worldwide television, Karr faced the cameras and stated that he was "with JonBenét when she died," that he loved her "very much," and he called her death an "accident."

The Yearbook

Within days, a sample of Karr's handwriting in a high school yearbook surfaced.

A handwriting expert appeared on CNN's *Larry King Live* to discuss similarities between the writing in the yearbook and the ransom note. He claimed that he saw "at least a dozen traits that match up perfectly." "Chances are a million to one," he asserted, that someone other than Karr wrote the ransom note.

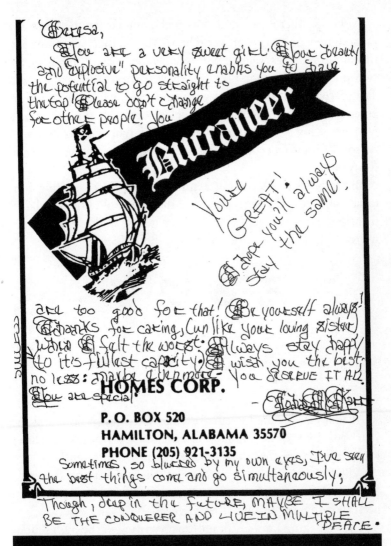

Theresa,

You are a very sweet girl! Your beauty and "explosive" personality enables you to have the potential to go straight to the top! Please don't change for other people! You

Buccaneer

You're GREAT! I hope you'll always stay the same!

are too good for that! Be yourself always! Thanks for caring, Cun like your loving sister) when I felt the worst. Always stay happy to it's fullest capacity. I wish you the best, no less: maybe even more. You deserve it all! You are special!

HOMES CORP.

P. O. BOX 520

HAMILTON, ALABAMA 35570

PHONE (205) 921-3135

Sometimes, so blurred by my own eyes, I've seen the best things come and go simultaneously;

Though, deep in the future, MAYBE I SHALL BE THE CONQUERER AND LIVE IN MULTIPLE PEACE.

ANGELICA FOREVERMORE..................
              Philosophy of a DREAMER,

Although there are some superficial similarities between the ransom note and the writing in the yearbook, there are many significant differences. One factor to remember when comparing the two documents is that they were written fourteen years apart. The yearbook inscription was written in 1982, when Karr was seventeen years old. The handwriting is consistent with that of a teenager who is experimenting with different writing styles. A person's writing can change a lot between the ages of seventeen and thirty-one.

But let's assume that fourteen years later, Karr's writing contained all of the elements we see in the yearbook. One similarity mentioned by some experts, and amateurs, is the use of typewriter-style *a*'s (with hoods on top) in both documents.

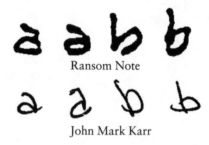

Ransom Note

John Mark Karr

At first glance, the lower-case *a*'s in the ransom note and the yearbook look quite similar. However, when you take a closer look, you can see that the letters were formed differently.

When comparing writing samples, there are many things to consider. You not only need to study individual letters, you also need to study the writing as a whole.

The first thing I notice about Karr's writing in the high school yearbook is that he flip-flops between very different handwriting styles. He combines highly decorative, printed, gothic-style letters with lower-case letters. Near the bottom of the page (which is more likely to be his natural style) he switches to an almost print-script writing (see the word "Though"). He also combines lower-case and upper-case letters in the words "futuRE" and "ANGELICy." And finally, he ends his message by writing in all capital letters. The handwriting on the ransom note has a more consistent and natural printing style than the writing in the yearbook.

"If you can't be famous, be infamous"

A week and a half after his arrest in Thailand, it became clear that John Mark Karr was not the intruder Boulder's district attorney had been looking for. Experts determined that Karr's DNA excluded him as a suspect. Despite Karr's insistence that he had accidentally killed JonBenét, investigators could find no physical evidence to link Karr to the crime. Moreover, interviews with Karr's family convinced prosecutors that it would have been impossible for Karr to have been in the Ramsey house on December 26, 1996, as he was more than a thousand miles away at the time.

Why does someone confess to a crime that he or she did not commit? Some people are so tormented by guilt over other aspects of their lives that they believe they deserve to be punished. Others are mentally ill or so delusional that they actually believe they committed the crime. Still others are motivated by a desire for their fifteen minutes of fame.

False confessions in high-profile cases are not all that rare. In the 1930s, more than two hundred people confessed to kidnapping the Lindbergh baby. At least six hundred people claimed to be the Black Dahlia killer, responsible for the 1947 murder of Elizabeth Short. A dozen people confessed to stabbing Nicole Brown Simpson and Ron Goldman to death in 1994. And don't forget about Laverne Pavlinac, whose false confession of the rape and murder of Taunja Bennett was so convincing that she and her boyfriend, John Sosnovske, spent five years in prison.

"Please don't let me be misunderstood"

Karr reportedly told a Thai official: "People say I am a monster and a horrible person. They don't know me." Let's look at his script and see if we can get to know him a little better.

Karr's yearbook inscription, with its elaborate, gothic-looking letters, has a hand-drawn, stylized look to it. As you learned in Chapter 8, this type of writing is known as "persona" or "facade" handwriting. You'll often see teenagers experiment with different facades as they try to "find themselves." Let's see what's hiding behind Karr's stylized script.

your

A conventional *y* loop will curve upward at the bottom. Look at the way Karr wrote the word "your." Do you see how the lower loop of the *y* curves downward forming a claw? As you'll recall from Chapter 6, this stroke is known as the "felon's claw." You'll find felon's claws in the handwriting of 80 percent of convicted felons. Felon's claw writers are experts at self-sabotage and self-destruction. They crave love and attention, but deep down they believe they don't deserve it, and ultimately they set themselves up for punishment and rejection.

(205) 921-
blurred ✝
come and

In Chapter 11, you learned that that when a lower-case *d* is distorted to the point of being unrecognizable, it is a sign of a writer with warped personal values. This includes ideas, morals, beliefs, and lifestyle. Isolate Karr's *d*'s by putting your hands around the surrounding letters. Could you tell that Karr's *d*'s were in fact *d*'s?

Karr virtually crosses out his personal pronoun "I." By obliterating his personal pronoun, Karr is symbolically eradicating his own personal identity.

Forensic psychiatrist Keith Ablow said this about Karr: "He seems untethered to his own existence. In other words, he's not sure of his own gender. He's not sure chronologically even what age he is. He had such a trauma in his early life experience, including apparently an assault, an attempted murder by his mother, that I think he is a free-floating individual who isn't anchored in himself."

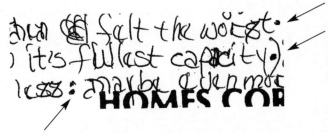

Karr went over his periods again and again, grinding them into the paper. As you saw in Chapter 12, these heavy, dark periods, known as "explosive dots," reveal that the writer is angry and irritable. According to one of Karr's former students: "[Karr] had a very nice side, and if you forgot your lunch money he'd give you a dollar. But he was always yelling and had a short fuse." Gorged dots also indicate that the writer is obsessive. After reading about the kidnapping and murder of 12-year-old Polly Klass, Karr became so obsessed with the case that he moved his family to her hometown of Petaluma, California.

Finally, look at the way Karr repeatedly underscored his signature. Many writers underline their signatures. A simple underline indicates that the writer is confident and has a healthy public self-image. However, when a writer underscores excessively, like Karr, it shows just the opposite.

The elaborate underlining in Karr's signature shows that he was overcompensating for feeling unimportant in the eyes of others. His writing shouts, "I don't want to be invisible. Notice me!" Willie Russell, who knew Karr in high school, recalls Karr saying, "Remember this face. I am going to be on every television in the world."

19

The Letter from Hell

Prologue

In the fall of 1888, five prostitutes were brutally murdered in London's East End. On August 31, 1888, the body of 43-year-old Polly Nichols was found in a gateway on Buck's Row. Her throat was slashed and there were deep cuts across her belly. On September 8, 1888, Annie Chapman, a 47-year-old widow, was discovered with her throat slashed behind a house on Hanbury Street. The killer's knife had made a deep, jagged cut all the way around her neck. Her intestines had been removed and laid across her left shoulder. Her killer had also cut out her uterus, and taken two brass rings from the middle finger of her left hand.

Three weeks later, on the night of September 30, 1888, the body of "Long Liz" Stride, forty-five, was found with her throat slashed near the International Worker's Club on Berner Street. Less than an hour later, Kate Eddowes's mutilated body was discovered in Mitre Square. Police calculated it would have taken the killer about eight minutes to walk there from Berner Street. Eddowes's killer had cut out her intestines and hacked off the right side of her face. Her uterus and left kidney were missing. At around 8 PM on the night of her death, the 43-year-old mother of three had made a scene outside the Bull Inn pub, about four blocks from Mitre Square, imitating a fire engine. After her drunken performance, she lay down in the street to sleep. She was last seen alive at around

1:00 AM, leaving the Bishopsgate Police Station, where she had been booked for public drunkenness and released.

On November 9, 1888, Mary Jane Kelly, twenty-five, also known as "Ginger," was found slaughtered in her own bed. The flesh on her face and body had been hacked to pieces, and her heart had been removed. Her uterus, kidneys, and one breast were found under her head. Her liver and other breast lay at her feet.

1889 British cartoon depicting Jack the Ripper

In the Whitechapel district of the East End, violence against women was not out of the ordinary, but these murders were different. It was clear to police and the public that most, if not all, of the murders were the work of one man. He was most likely left-handed, had some medical knowledge and skill . . . and was likely to strike again.

As Scotland Yard searched desperately for clues, the police, local authorities, and the press received more than 700 letters—all hoaxes, except for one: an anonymous letter with a most unusual return address: "from hell."

The Letter from Hell

A tall man wrapped in a long black cloak handed the package to the postal clerk. "Good day, sir," the clerk uttered as he placed the three-inch-square cardboard box in the back with the rest of the mail.

On October 16, 1888, George Lusk received the box in the mail. Lusk, a builder, had recently been elected chairman of the Whitechapel Vigilance Committee (a new group formed to patrol the district's streets). In the box was a letter, wrapped around a half of a kidney.

From hell

Mr Lusk
      Sir
I send you half the Kidne I took from one women prasarved it for you tother piece I fried and ate it was very nise I may send you the bloody knif that took it out if you only wate a whil longer
      Signed
                  Catch me when
                              You can
                              Mishter Lusk.

"This must be a joke," Lusk thought, "Surely it's not the kidney of a person." But when he showed the contents of the box to another committee member, he was persuaded to take the organ to a doctor. Just two weeks prior, Lusk recalled, Kate Eddowes had been murdered in Mitre Square. Her body had been mutilated, her uterus and left kidney removed. "Could this be the kidney of poor Kate Eddowes?" Lusk asked Dr. Openshaw.

George Akin Lusk, Chairman of
the Whitechapel Vigilance Committee

Dr. Thomas Openshaw, chief pathologist at London Hospital, concluded that the organ was a large fraction of a human kidney, consistent with the left kidney of a woman approximately forty-five years of age.

After examining the organ, Dr. Sutton, a senior surgeon of London Hospital and one of the world's leading kidney authorities, told Sir Henry Smith, the City of London Police Commissioner, "that he would pledge his reputation that the kidney . . . had been put in spirits within a few hours of removal from the body, thus," in Smith's opinion, "effectually disposing of all hoaxes in connection with it."

In his memoirs, Smith described the results of an analysis by the City's medical examiner: "The renal artery is about three inches long. Two inches remained in the corpse, one inch was attached to the kidney. The kidney left in the corpse was in an advanced stage of Bright's Disease; the kidney sent me was in an exactly similar state."

Since the kidney sent to Lusk was almost certainly part of the kidney that had been removed from Kate Eddowes, Smith concluded, the letter "from hell" was almost certainly written by the killer.

What kind of man—or woman—wrote the letter? Let's compare the letter "from hell" to another letter turned over to police a few weeks earlier.

On September 27, 1888, the Central News Agency received a letter addressed to "the Boss." It was this letter, signed "Jack the Ripper," that gave the killer his unforgettable name.

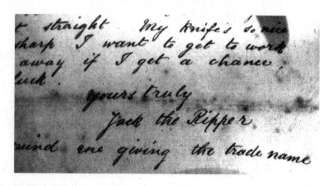

The police posted copies of the "Dear Boss" letter, along with a postcard received four days later, outside every police station, in the hope that someone would recognize the handwriting. The papers reprinted the text of the letters, which fueled newspaper sales and the growing panic. But instead of leads, the police received stacks and stacks of copycat letters. Each letter had to be analyzed and investigated, wasting valuable time and resources.

Two Letters, Two Hands

If you compare the "Dear Boss" and "from hell" letters, you will see significant differences in their sentence structure, legibility, level of sophistication, and in the way individual letters are formed. And there's a huge difference in the amount of space each writer leaves between words.

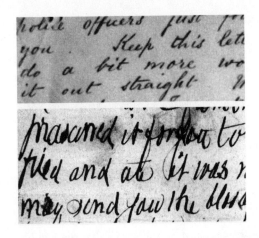

The writer of the "Dear Boss" letter had an organized, neat, and flowing script. It is the writing of a rational, educated, and organized writer, whose actions were well thought out and planned. His *i* dots were well formed and always placed neatly and precisely above the stem. Exact *i* dots show that the writer was precise, particular, and had an eye for detail.

As you'll recall, the letters *o* and *a* are the communication letters. The "Dear Boss" author made his *o*'s and *a*'s clearly and crisply, with absolutely no clutter inside them. These exceptionally clean *o*'s and *a*'s show that the writer was a skilled communicator.

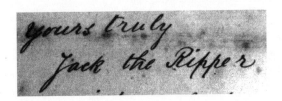

The personality characteristics evident in the handwriting of the "Dear Boss" letter are the opposite of what we would expect in the handwriting of a disorganized lust murderer. However, they do fit an organized, ambitious, detail-oriented writer—someone sharp enough to pull off a hoax that could fool people for over 100 years. Could the author have been a professional writer?

Scotland Yard thought so. Scotland Yard's Chief Inspector, John George Littlechild, confided to a friend that in his opinion, the letter was cooked up by the Central News Agency's "Boss" himself, John Moore.

A Dangerous Mind

The Whitechapel murders were done in a fit of passion. The murderer's rage escalated quickly and uncontrollably. The frenzied way the killer multilated his victims and removed their sex organs indicates that he was prone to erotic mania, was sexually incompetent, and was consumed with a deep hostility towards women. The FBI classifies this type of offender as a disorganized lust murderer.

The letter from hell contains a number of "red flags" that are often associated with a disorganized lust killer:

Red flag #1: Angled circle letters. As we saw in Chapter 1, when a writer is overexcited, aggressive, hostile, or angry, his muscles become tight and tense. This makes it difficult to form curves, and the handwriting takes on a stiff, angular appearance. Look at the *o* in the word "From." Do you see how it is squeezed and angular? When letters that are normally curved and rounded become angular, it indicates that the writer is unsympathetic, crude, and cruel.

Sample A is from the letter "from hell." Sample B is the writing of Nazi official Heinrich Himmler, head of the SS and Gestapo.

Red flag #2: The *F* in "From" starts with a checkmark-like stroke. Strokes that look like check marks are known as ticks. Ticks show rage, hostility, irritability, and frustration. Tick writers have short fuses and can lose their tempers at the drop of a hat. The heavier the pressure on the tick, the more likely the writer will fly off the handle.

A   B   C

Sample A is from the letter "from hell." Sample B is the signature of John Wilkes Booth, who assassinated President Lincoln. Sample C is the writing of serial killer Dennis Nilsen.

Red flag #3: Angular lower loops. As you'll recall from Chapter 2, the lower zone of the bottom loops of the letters f, g, j, p, q, and y correlates to the writer's sexual fantasies, desires, and drives. When you see angular loops in a writer's lower zone, it's a sign that the writer has deep-rooted rage that is likely to be expressed in sexual violence or aggression. Take a good look at the lower zones in the letter "from hell." Notice the sharp, angular lower loops of the y's in "only" and "bloody."

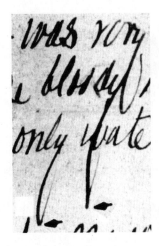

Red flag #4: Dark, ink-filled circle letters. Ink-filled circle letters (*a*'s, *o*'s, and *e*'s) show a writer with compulsive, dark, and morbid thoughts—a writer who cannot control his libidinal urges. Notice the dark and muddied *o*'s in the word "bloody."

Sample A: The letter "from hell"; Sample B: Writing of conman/murderer Kenneth Kimes; Sample C: Writing of serial killer David Berkowitz ("Son of Sam")

Red flag #5: Weapon formations. Often, a killer's weapon of choice can be seen in his handwriting. Notice how: 1) the bottom left of the *f* in "From" and *S* in "Sir" resemble curved knives or sabers, and 2) the lower loops of the letter *f* in "haf" and the letter *y* in the words "only" and "bloody" look like sharp daggers or scalpels. The Whitechapel murderer is believed to have used two types of knives, one dagger-like and one saber-like, to kill his victims.

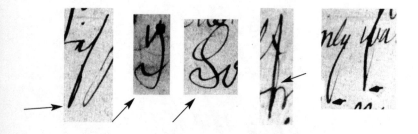

Red flag #6: Exaggerated lower zone. An elongated or exaggerated lower zone indicates that the writer has overwhelming sexual desires and fantasies. The longer or more exaggerated the loops, the more he is compelled to violate sexual taboos.

Compare the lower loops in the letter from hell (Sample A) with those of Ted Bundy (Sample B). Notice how both writers' loops are so long that they invade the space of the lines below. Writers with exaggerated lower loops cannot stay within society's sexual boundaries.

A   B

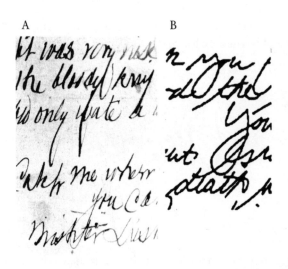

Red flag #7: Ambiguous letters. When you see lots of ambiguous or "trick" letters, you're looking at the handwriting of a liar or con artist.

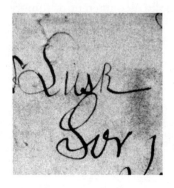

"Lusk" could read "SusR." "Sir" could be "Sor" or possibly "Fur" or "Sur" or "For."

FBI research shows that there are a number of key traits that distinguish disorganized murderers from organized murderers. Three of these traits appear in the handwriting of the letter "from hell."

Anxiousness. The extra loop in the letter *n* in the word "signed" is a worry loop. It shows that the writer was worried and anxious.

Sexual incompetence. Broken lower loops indicate that a person has had some type of trauma—physical or emotional—relating to their sexual organs, sex life, or lower body. Do you see the gap in the lower loop of the *y* in the word "you"? This break indicates that the "from hell" writer was sexually incompetent or impotent.

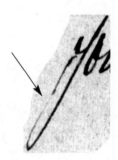

Mania. Manic writers will have handwriting that travels uphill. The lines in the letter "from hell" ascend more and more as the letter continues. His upward script shows the writer was manic, while his exaggerated lower loops show the erotic component of his mania. The slope of a bipolar writer's handwriting will fluctuate with his mood. At the time he wrote this letter, the killer was in a manic, erotic state. It is likely that when the writer was in a depressed state, his handwriting followed, and sloped noticeably downhill.

"Catch me when you can"

The handwriting on the letter "from hell" is perfectly consistent with the handwriting of a dangerous, mentally and sexually disturbed individual—someone who is angry and explosively violent, and whose weapon of choice is a knife or dagger. It is not the handwriting of a prankster. It is the handwriting of a man who fits the precise profile of Jack the Ripper.

Background and Education

Ripperologists have long debated whether the murderer was an immigrant. Sir Robert Anderson, who in 1888 was Assistant Commissioner of London's Metropolitan Police, was convinced the Whitechapel murderer was a Jewish immigrant, as he wrote in his memoirs: "The conclusion we came to was that (the Ripper) and his people were low-class Jews, for it is a remarkable fact that people of that class in the East End will not give up one of their number to Gentile justice."

In late-nineteenth-century London, most "low-class" Jewish immigrants spoke and wrote little if any English. Their primary language was Yiddish.

Contractions like "tother" for "the other" were common in England, Scotland, America, and Ireland. "Prasarved" suggests that the writer spoke Cockney or Irish English. The word

"Mishter" was also used in Cockney and Irish English, where the *sh* sound was commonly substituted for *s*.

Retired FBI profiler John Douglas believes that the writing in the letter "from hell" is that of someone unfamiliar with the English language, an uneducated immigrant writing phonetically. I disagree. If the words were spelled the way they sounded, "knife," "half," and "while" would be spelled "nif," "haf," and "wile." not "knif," "half," and "whil."

The writer had some formal schooling in English because he followed the basic structure of a formal letter. However, his education was limited, as he did not know how to use punctuation or capitalization correctly. And his spelling was, to say the least, lousy.

A Closer Look

As we saw in Chapter 1, you can learn quite a lot about a writer from his personal pronoun "I." There are two different types of personal pronouns in the letter:

A   B

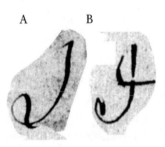

- The first I (A) has a short, angular mother stroke and a down-turned father loop. The incomplete mother stroke shows that the writer's mother did not play a significant role in his life. The mother stroke forms a tick mark, which shows that the writer still has anger toward his mother. The distorted father loop shows that, while he had a relationship with his father, it was strained.

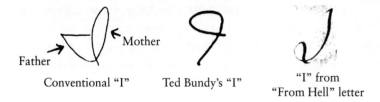

Father · Mother · Conventional "I"   Ted Bundy's "I"   "I" from
"From Hell" letter

Ted Bundy never knew his biological father. Notice that his "I" has no father loop.

- In the second "I" (B), the mother stroke is split in two. This is a sign that the writer had a "split" personality. The father loop ends with a sharp, downturned tick mark, suggesting the writer had anger toward his father.

A   B

Compare the split "I" in the letter "from hell" with David Berkowitz's split "I" (B).

The narrow spacing between his words indicates that the writer had a fear of abandonment.

The handwriting looks dirty, muddied, and smudged. I would expect the writer to appear unkempt, dressed in dirty, nondescript clothing.

The thick lines, irregular pressure, blotchy i dots, and numerous smears show that the writer was suffering from a chronic illness.

The script is large and bold, which indicates that the writer saw himself as something of a big shot. As killers go, the writer was a social person, not a recluse. But it's likely that he revealed little of his true self to others. Notice that the tops of his communication letters o and a are completely closed, a sign of a secretive personality.

If you look closely, you will see that the writer made some of his lower loops on the left side of the stem and some on the right side. Writers with lower loops that "swing both ways" are consumed with sexual fantasies about both men and women.

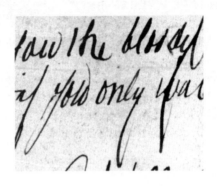

Prime Suspects

From a single handwritten letter, we've learned quite a few things about the mysterious Ripper:

1. He spoke with a Cockney or Irish accent.
2. He had a brief or insignificant relationship with his mother.
3. He had a strained relationship with his father.
4. He was an extrovert.
5. He had extreme sexual anger.
6. He was bisexual.
7. He was violent.
8. He had a fear of abandonment.
9. He was semiliterate, with a rudimentary, grade-school education.
10. He had a chronic illness.
11. He was unkempt and had a nondescript, dirty appearance.

Let's compare our profile to the prime suspects.

Walter Sickert

In her bestselling book *Portrait of a Killer: Jack the Ripper, Case Closed,* Patricia Cornwell asserts that the Ripper was Walter Sickert, an eccentric British painter born to an English mother and Danish father in Munich, Germany.

In 1908, Sickert painted a series of grisly paintings depicting the murder of a Camden prostitute. Cornwell claims that these paintings were, in fact, images of the Ripper's victims, images only the killer could paint. "This painter never painted anything he had not seen," Cornwell stated.

But I know, as an artist, that paintings are not documentary evidence. Painters find inspiration from many, many sources, real and imaginary. Just because Sickert imagined what it was like to be the Ripper doesn't mean he actually was the Ripper.

Cornwell was so determined to prove her case that she reportedly spent over $3 million on her investigation of Sickert. She bought thirty-two of his paintings, destroying one (considered a masterpiece) in search of evidence. She hired a team of experts to compare traces of DNA on Ripper letters with traces on DNA on letters written by Sickert. Her experts found a partial match in the mitochondrial DNA from a single Ripper letter with Sickert's mitochondrial DNA, and matched watermarks on Ripper letters to watermarks on stationery used by Sickert. "It is obvious," she writes, "that the actual Ripper wrote far more of the Ripper letters than he has ever been credited with. In fact, I believe that he wrote most of them."

Even if Sickert wrote several hundred Ripper letters, as Cornwell claims, he didn't write the letter "from hell," which is the only Ripper letter written by the killer. If anything, Cornwell may have made a case that Sickert—who wrote hundreds of letters to newspapers during his lifetime—was a brilliant hoaxster.

Aaron Kosminski

In 1998, John Douglas and Roy Hazelwood, two top FBI profilers, were featured on a television program called *The Secret Identity of Jack the Ripper*. Using modern-day profiling techniques, each profiler assessed the major suspects. Working independently, they both arrived at the same conclusion: Jack the Ripper was most likely a poor Jewish immigrant named Aaron Kosminski. Kosminski had emigrated from Poland to England in 1882. He was identified as the killer by an eyewitness two years after the murders—even though Kosminski looked nothing like the witness's original description.

At age twenty-four, Aaron Kosminski was confined to a lunatic asylum, where he remained for the next twenty-eight years. His diagnosis read: "chronic harmless lunatic, idiot or imbecile."

It is highly unlikely that a poor Jewish immigrant like Kosminski, for whom English would have been a second or third language, could have authored the letter "from hell" or anything like it. Based on the handwriting evidence, Aaron Kosminski could not have been Jack the Ripper.

Prince Eddy

A number of authors have argued that Prince Albert Victor Christian Edward, duke of Clarence (Prince Eddy), Queen Victoria's eldest grandson, was either Jack the Ripper or at the center of a royal conspiracy to murder East End prostitutes who "knew too much" about the prince's illicit activities. There is little evidence to support either of these theories.

Prince Eddy, though he may have been a fool, was an educated fool who certainly does not fit the profile of the semiliterate writer of the letter "from hell." As for the royal conspiracy theory, none of the alleged conspirators fit the "from hell" writer's profile, either. Besides, assuming that the prince or one or more royal conspirators did murder five prostitutes, why would they write to a local community leader like George Lusk? The answer is: they didn't and they wouldn't.

Severin Klosowski

Severin Klosowski trained as a surgeon's assistant in Poland before emigrating to England in 1887. By 1888, now calling himself George Chapman, he was a modestly successful hairdresser and barber in Whitechapel. Not considered a suspect at the time, Klosowski was later convicted of poisoning three of his common-law wives. When details of his past were revealed during his 1903 trial (including his extensive criminal activities and pattern of violence against women, and the fact that in the fall of 1888 he lived in Whitechapel) some—including Inspector Frederick Abberline, the lead investigator assigned to the Ripper case—came to believe that Klosowski was the Ripper.

Klosowski was a patient and organized killer, who calmly watched his common-law wives die painful deaths from his poison. Along with bombers, poisoners are the most deliberate and detached killers. Their handwriting is usually painfully slow, precise, and mechanical looking.

Klosowski may have been a woman-hater and a cruel, cold psychopath, but Klosowki was not the Ripper.

James Maybrick

James Maybrick was a successful Liverpool cotton trader. He was not considered a suspect in the Whitechapel murders until 1993, when a book purporting to be Maybrick's diary was published. The diary told how Maybrick had led a secret life as a serial killer. The last page was signed: "yours truly, Jack the Ripper." Handwriting experts who have examined the diary have concluded that it does not match any of Maybrick's known writing and is likely a fake. The handwriting of the diary does not match the handwriting of the letter "from hell" either, nor does the personality of the diary's supposed author match the profile of the killer. The evidence also indicates that whoever wrote the diary probably did so in several sittings, rather than writing it over a period of time. Finally, Michael Barrett, the Liverpool scrap-metal dealer who sold the diary to the publisher, now claims that the document is a fake. How does he know? He says he wrote it himself.

Francis Tumblety

John George Littlechild, Chief of Scotland Yard's Special Branch at the time of the murders, considered Dr. Francis Tumblety "a very likely suspect," observing that after he left England "the Ripper murders came to an end."

During the summer of 1888, Scotland Yard was keeping an eye on an American quack who called himself the "Indian Herb Doctor." For nearly twenty years, Francis Tumblety was a well-known figure to police in both Liverpool and London, where there had been numerous complaints about his homosexual activities with young men.

After the double murder of Liz Stride and Kate Eddowes on September 30, the landlady of a boardinghouse on Batty Street contacted the police. One of her lodgers, an American doctor, had returned to his room in the early morning hours of October 1, just minutes after Kate Eddowes's body was discovered in Mitre Square, a few blocks away. The doctor changed his clothing and left a short time later. When the landlady found a blood-stained shirt in his room, she was convinced that Tumblety must be the "Whitechapel fiend."

Tumblety was arrested on November 7 on charges of indecent assault against four young men. "Indecent assault" was a euphemism for "homosexual acts." But these acts had apparently been violent, as the charges included "assault with force and arms." On November 12, prosecutors appeared before a judge with charges that Tumblety was connected with the Whitechapel murders. The judge set Tumblety's bail at 300 pounds (around $1,500), a

figure high enough, it was thought, to keep the Indian Herb Doctor in jail, while police interviewed more witnesses and gathered
more evidence against him.

But on November 16, Tumblety made bail, and a few days
later, Scotland Yard's leading suspect fled the country. He arrived
in Le Havre, France on November 24, traveling under the alias
"Frank Townsend."

In New York, a week later, as "Frank Townsend" made his
way down the gangplank of the French steamer *Bretagne,* he
appeared nervous. On the ship, he had been keeping a low profile,
rarely leaving his cabin, even for meals. There was a crowd waiting for him at the pier, including a cadre of reporters and dozens
of police officers. Tumblety ducked into a cab and headed toward
a boardinghouse on the Lower East Side. On December 4, 1888,
the *New York World* newspaper declared:

TUMBLETY IS IN THIS CITY
HE ARRIVED SUNDAY UNDER A FALSE NAME
FROM FRANCE
**A Big English Detective Is Watching Him Closely, and
a Crowd of Curious People Gaze at the House He Lives In**

Apparently the Big English Detective wasn't watching Tumblety
very closely. The next morning, Tumblety walked down the
block, boarded an uptown streetcar, and disappeared into obscurity. English papers said nothing about the man who got away.
And all traces of Tumblety, including handwriting samples
obtained from his bank in San Francisco, mysteriously disappeared from Scotland's Yard's case files.

In April 1903, Tumblety appeared at the door of St. John's
Charity hospital in St. Louis, Missouri looking for a place to die.
He registered under the name "Frank Townsend," the same name
he had used in 1888, as he fled England for America. When he died
in May 1903, Francis Tumblety's estate was valued at more than
$135,000, a sizable sum in 1903. Among his personal effects, in
addition to fine gold and diamond rings and a gold pocket watch,

were two brass rings matching the description of the rings missing from Annie Chapman, the Ripper's second victim.

A Match Made in Hell

Francis Tumblety fits the writer "from hell's" profile in a startling number of ways:

The writer spoke with a Cockney or Irish accent.
- Tumblety was born in Ireland in 1833, the youngest of eleven children. A few years later, the family moved to Rochester, New York.

The writer had a brief or insignificant relationship with his mother.
- One childhood acquaintance described young Francis Tumblety as a "dirty, awkward, ignorant, uncared-for, good-for-nothing boy." His mother, Margaret Tumblety, sent Francis to live with his brother when he was eleven.

The writer had a strained relationship with his father.
- Little is known about Tumblety's relationship with his father, James. James Tumblety passed away soon after Francis left Rochester, at the age of seventeen.

The writer was bisexual.
- After Tumblety's failed marriage to a prostitute, he leaned towards young men. One of his lovers was Hall Caine, a young writer in Liverpool, who later in life became a best-selling romance novelist. (Caine was a confidant and mentor to Bram Stoker, and is the man to whom Stoker dedicated his novel *Dracula*.)

The writer had a fear of abandonment.
- Through his twenties and thirties, Tumblety was scarcely seen by his family and rarely stayed in one place for long.

Yet as he grew older, he began to spend more time with his sisters. During the 1870s and 1880s, he often stayed with a sister who lived in Liverpool, England. Letters to Hall Caine during this period had a desperate tone. Tumblety pleaded with Caine to return with him to America. In 1893, Tumblety moved in with his sister and niece in Rochester, New York.

The writer was an extrovert.

- Old acquaintances described how the self-promoting charlatan would call attention to himself after arriving in a new city by parading through the center of town, dressed in a medal-festooned uniform, and followed by a valet and two greyhounds. As an energetic hustler who advertised heavily in local newspapers, Tumblety made a small fortune.

- One New York acquaintance recalled that during the 1870s, Tumblety "cordially invited any young men whom he fancied, wherever he met them, in the parks, squares or stores, to call upon him at this hotel, where he was wont to say he would show them 'an easy road to fortune.'"

The writer had extreme sexual anger.

- Tumblety was regarded as a misogynist. There are numerous accounts of Tumblety's "bitter hatred of women." A lawyer representing the mother of a young man Tumblety had once employed told a reporter: "I had a big batch of letters sent by him to the young man . . . and they were the most amusing farrago of illiterate nonsense . . . He never failed to warn his correspondents against lewd women, and in doing it used the most shocking language."

- Interestingly, many of Tumblety's patients were the very same lewd women he despised. In Montreal, when a young prostitute in Montreal died after an abortion in 1857, Tumblety was tried and acquitted. (A few years later in St. John, New Brunswick, Tumblety was convicted of manslaughter. Tumblety jumped bail and fled to America before sentencing.)

- Colonel C. A. Dunham, a prominent Washington attorney, reported that when Tumblety "was asked why he hated women, he said that when quite a young man he fell desperately in love with a pretty girl, rather his senior, who promised to reciprocate his affection. After a brief courtship he married her. The honeymoon was not over when he noticed a disposition on the part of his wife to flirt with other men. He remonstrated, she kissed him, called him a dear, jealous fool—and he believed her. Happening to pass one day in a cab through the worst part of the town he saw his wife and a man enter a gloomy looking house. Then he learned that before her marriage his wife had been an inmate of that and many similar houses. Then he gave up on all womankind."
- Dunham also reported that Tumblety kept a collection of women's uteruses in glass jars, which, he liked to brag, came from "every class of women." It is believed that Tumblety acquired much of his collection as the result of botched abortions. The Whitechapel murderer cut out and took the uteruses of two of his victims, Annie Chapman and Kate Eddowes.

The writer was violent.
- Tumblety was arrested in London for "indecent assault with force and arms," which suggests that he violently attacked his victims. Witnesses have described Tumblety's violent temper. In one incident, Tumblety was arrested for assaulting an editor in a New York hotel with a cane. Apparently, the editor had printed an article about Tumblety's murder trial in Canada a decade earlier.

He was semiliterate, with a rudimentary, grade-school education.
- Tumblety attended only a few years of grade school.
- "He was utterly devoid of education," said one childhood

acquaintance from Rochester. "He lived with his brother, who was my uncle's gardener. The only training he ever had for the medical profession was a little drugstore at the back of the Arcade, which was kept by Doctor Lispenard, who carried on a medical business of a disreputable kind."

The writer had a chronic illness.
- Hospital records indicate that Tumblety suffered from chronic nephritis and "valvular disease of the heart."

The writer was unkempt and had a nondescript, dirty appearance.
- Clement R. Bennett, a well-known stenographer in the New York Circuit Court, met Tumblety in 1870, when he was impressed by Tumblety's "dash and hauteur." But when Bennett ran into Tumblety in 1879, "he was then looking shabby, careworn, lame, appeared to be living a dissolute and dissipated life, and was begging for a night's lodging."

The writer was a liar or con artist.
- Tumblety was a con artist who went by many aliases including Frank Townsend, Frank Tumilty, Francis Twomblety, J. J. Blackburn, W. J. Morgan and Michael Sullivan. He lived his life as an impostor, pretending to be an "Indian Herb Doctor," a decorated medical officer with the US Army, and a confidant of presidents, queens, and emperors.
- Tumblety reportedly made much of his money selling his bottled miracle cures, which, he claimed, were made from a combination of secret herbs and spices he learned from a Native American medicine man. In a number of cases, Tumblety's miracle cure turned out to be deadly. Tumblety's secret concoction of herbs, spices, and alcohol was highly poisonous. This may explain the Herb Doctor's frequent changes of name and address.

Contemporary cartoon of Tumblety's
1865 arrest in America on suspicion
of plotting to infect Union troops
with yellow fever.

From One Hand T'other

Francis Tumblety fits the profile of the writer from hell like a
bloody glove. But does his handwriting match the handwriting on
the letter "from hell"? Here are two known samples of Tumblety's writing.

The first is a letter he wrote to Hall Caine in 1875 when Tumblety was living in Liverpool, England. The second is Tumblety's
signature from a will he signed in St. Louis, Missouri in 1903,
shortly before he died. The first sample was written thirteen
years before the letter "from hell," while the second sample was
written fifteen years afterwards.

Both the letter "from hell" and Tumblety's letter are totally devoid of punctuation. By writing continuously, without commas, periods, dashes, or hesitation of any kind, the writer is saying "Stop me if you can, because I won't stop myself . . ."

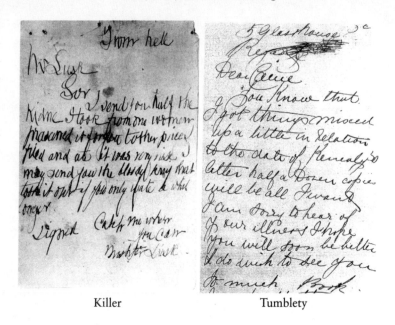

Killer   Tumblety

Let's take a closer look at Tumblety's known writing and the writing of the killer. Both scripts contain huge lowercase *a*'s (which are large relative to the letters around them). Compare the large, out-of-proportion *a* in the killer's word "prasarved" to Tumblety's *a* in the word "Caine." Both scripts also contain little baby *a*'s (which are small relative to the surrounding letters). Compare the teeny *a* in the killer's word "and" to the wee *a* in the word "Dear."

Killer   Tumblety

Both the killer and Tumblety make two types of *k*'s. The first type employs a capital *K* where a lowercase *k* should be. Notice the out-of-place capital *K*'s in the killer's "Kidney" and in Tumblety's "Know." Both writers insert a little loop in the center, where the two parts of the *K* connect.

Killer   Tumblety

The second type of *k*, in the killer's "knif" and "took" and in Tumblety's "book," resembles a capital *R*.

Killer   Tumblety

The loops in the lower case *d*'s in both scripts are disconnected from the stem of the *d*. Some *d*'s resemble the letters *ol*, while some loops are open at the top, making the *d* look like *cl*.

Killer   Tumblety

There are three types of *h*'s in each writer's script. Look at the strong similarities.

Killer   Tumblety

In both scripts, the letter *e* is vertical, ink-filled, and relatively small compared to the other letters.

Killer   Tumblety

When a writer leaves a large gap between the up and down strokes of a letter stem, it creates a "split." Notice the unusual splits in many of the lowercase letters written by the killer and Tumblety.

Killer   Tumblety

Both writers have similar, unconventional word connections.

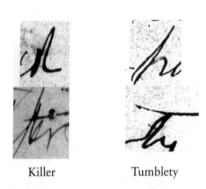

Killer   Tumblety

Both writers are in the habit of making their *t* bars with a strong emphasis on the right side of the stem.

Now, pay special attention to the *o*'s in the bottom samples. See how they're the same oval shape? And notice how both are open at the top and have the same little top connecting loop to the letter that follows.

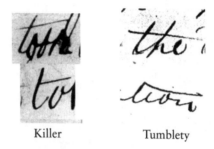

Killer   Tumblety

Both Tumblety and the killer make two types of lowercase *p*'s. One type is open at the bottom, like an *n*. The other type is closed. Notice how the closed *p*'s have a similar, oval shape.

Killer   Tumblety

Both writers have many broken lower loops, a sign of impotence or sexual incompetence.

Killer   Tumblety

Both writers alternate between making their lower loops on the right and left of the stem, a sign of bisexuality.

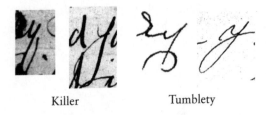

Killer   Tumblety

Compare the letter *M* in the "Mr" and the letter *D* in "Dr." Both initial strokes have a slight curve and start high above the rest of the letter.

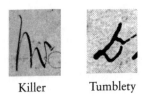

Killer   Tumblety

Tumblety's three types of lowercase *r*'s can all be found in the "from hell" letter. The *r*'s in "prasarved," "sorry," and "hear" have little loops at the top left.

Killer   Tumblety

Like the lower loops in the letter "from hell," the lower loops in Tumblety's letter are exceptionally long, invading the line below, a sign of a writer who ignores society's sexual boundaries.

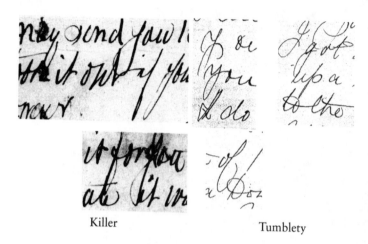

Killer   Tumblety

Both scripts have an unusually large variety of upper and lower case s's. In both letters, lower and upper case letters are used interchangeably. Look carefully, and you will see a number of similarities between s's in the killer's writing and in Tumblety's writing.

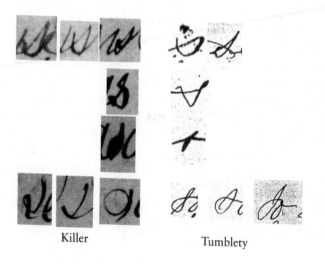

Killer   Tumblety

Both writers make their lower case o's with a loop at the top, with similar variations.

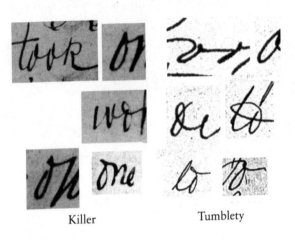

Killer   Tumblety

Tumble-who?

Several years ago, on Halloween night, I joined twenty other curious souls on a "Molly's Trolleys Fright Night Tour." As our bright red trolley ventured into Pittsburgh's spooky, historic dark side, our tour guide pointed out a run-down Victorian house that was home to a doctor in the late 1800s. This doctor had a secret specialty. He performed abortions. A number of girls, too embarrassed to tell their families about their plight, met the doctor at his home in the middle of the night. They were never seen again, and no one knew what had become of them until one young lady confided to her roommate that she was planning to visit the doctor that evening. When she didn't return home, her roommate went to the police. By the time the police showed up at his house, the doctor was gone. But he had left behind a number of "souvenirs." Sitting on the shelves of a cupboard were dozens of jars filled with uteruses, kidneys, and other body parts.

The following October, while visiting London, I went on a midnight walking tour of the East End. As we wandered through the dark alleys of Whitechapel, in the footsteps of Jack the Ripper, our guide told us the gory details of each Ripper murder.

When I decided to write this chapter on Jack the Ripper, my goal was to explain why the "from hell" letter was not a hoax letter but an actual letter written by the Whitechapel killer. I had intended to explore some of the main Ripper suspects and go a little into their backgrounds. I figured that I would end the chapter with something like, "We may never know the real identity of the Whitechapel murderer." But as I pored over old articles and books on the prime suspects, I kept coming back to a questionable character whom I had never heard of before—Dr. Francis Tumblety. I knew there was something about this strange man that was strangely familiar.

Then it hit me: That spooky house in Pittsburgh was Tumblety's house. And the path of Jack the Ripper in London was the path that Tumblety walked!

Indeed, Francis Tumblety hung his shingle in Pittsburgh many times. His last stint in Pittsburgh was short. He must have sensed that the police were onto him, because he disappeared very suddenly, leaving in the middle of night, leaving behind his treasured specimen cabinet, and not even a forwarding address.

It might have been the same story in London. But in the fall of 1888, as Francis Tumblety fled the city he had terrorized for three months, he left behind a letter. And that letter did have a forwarding address: "from hell."

The handwriting in the letter "from hell" matches Tumblety's bizarre personality trait by trait, and matches Tumblety's bizarre handwriting, stroke for stroke. And it proves, with a high degree of professional certainty, that Francis Tumblety was the cold-blooded killer known as Jack the Ripper.

PART V

Let's Get Personal

20

⌒

The Truth, the Whole Truth, and Nothing But . . .

In 1999, I began writing "The Handwriting Doctor," a syndi-cated column in which I use my skills as a handwriting profiler to give readers insights into themselves, their personal issues, and their interactions with others. Over the years, I've received many incredibly candid letters from readers all over the world. You've already seen some of their writing in earlier chapters. In this chapter, I'll share with you the insights and advice I gave these writers based on their actual handwriting.

The Hitting Girl

Dear Michelle,
    I would like to know about me and stuff. I don't get along with my mom. We get into fights a lot. And I can't be around my brother. I just want to hit them sometimes. I get mad and anything anybody does or says makes me feel like just punching them. Why do I do that and how can I stop it?

                    Thank you,
                    Your friend from Quincy

I would like to know about me and stuff I don't get along with my mom all the time we get into fights a lot and I cant be around my [mother] I jus[t]

Dear Friend,

Muhammad Ali once said, "I make a good living beating people up." For the rest of us, however, communicating with our fists can only get us into a heap of trouble.

You may lash out because you feel like your life is going in the wrong direction. How do I know that? I took one look at your personal pronoun "I." It's backwards! The capital *I* is the one letter in the English alphabet that is a very important word. The word "I" stands for you . . . and the way you make it shows how you feel about yourself. Your backwards *I* tells me that you need to get a clearer, more positive self-image and start back in the right direction.

Your upper zone—the top loops in the letters *b, d, f, h, k,* and *l*—correlates to your head and thinking processes. Notice that many of your upper loops are tight and squished. Sometimes they are so pinched at the top that they come to a point. These squished upper loops reflect a desire to squish out the thoughts that are in your head and hide your true feelings.

To "knock out" some of your tension I recommend that you try something called "handwriting therapy."

Keep a journal and write down your feelings in it every day. See if you can make your upper loops less tense by relaxing your hand and your mind. Also, concentrate on making your personal pronoun "I" in the right direction. At the same time, say to yourself: "I know who I am and I know the direction I want to go in my life."

By changing the way you write, you can actually send signals to your brain that will help change the way you think and feel about "stuff."

Concerned Grandma

Dear Michelle,

My 11-year-old grandson lives with my husband and me during the school week. He has had problems with learning and with other children. His mom felt our school district was better for him. He hates to read and feels that adults should help him with his homework. He is bossy and sometimes mean to his younger brother. He can also be rather aggressive to adult males. When he changed schools he was put back a grade, however we think he resists learning. He says that he doesn't want to grow up.

His father has never been a father in any way except for conception. When his father does see him . . . he plays adult mind games on him and criticizes him mercilessly.

How can we help this boy become more cheerful and want to learn and play with other children and ultimately become a nice adult? I am enclosing a copy of one of his school papers. Thanks for anything you can point out.

Concerned Grandmother in Chicago

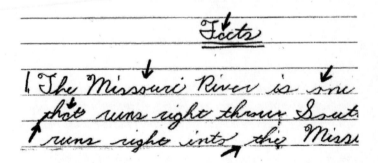

Dear Grandma,

If the first button of one's coat is buttoned wrong, all the rest will be crooked. The same goes for people. Let's look at your grandson's handwriting to see what's behind his difficult behavior.

His writing has two significant "no-no" traits: resentment strokes and disguised letters. Look at the straight lead-in stroke at the beginning of words "that" and "the." This is a resentment stroke, and it indicates that your grandson has deep, unresolved anger. Given his father's behavior, it's not surprising that your grandson has resentment strokes throughout his writing.

Disguised letters are letters that appear to be something they are not. For example, taken out of context, the *a*'s in "Facts" and "that" look like *c*'s and the *o*'s in "Missouri" and "one" could easily be mistaken for *s*'s. Disguised letters are common in the writing of criminals, and are usually indicators of a manipulative and deceptive personality. However, in a child's writing, ambiguous letters can also indicate a learning disability.

Your grandson needs counseling. I strongly recommend that he see a therapist who specializes in treating children. He should also be tested for learning disabilities.

You obviously care very much for your grandson and want to see him on the right path. Don't wait to get help. Now is the time to straighten him out.

Nosedive

Greetings Michelle,

My brother and I recently lost our mom and dad. As a result, I have been distracted, forgetful, unambitious . . . just not myself. Does my handwriting reflect these listless feelings and lack of direction? Does it point to anything inherent in my character or personality to pulling out of this nosedive and flying higher?

Thank you, Daniel from Portland, Oregon

Dear Daniel,

Let's look at your handwriting to see how we can create an updraft and get you flying on a higher plain.

The English language is written from left to right. The left side of the page represents where we came from (our past), while the right side of the page represents where we're going (our future). Notice that when you write a *t* at the end of a word, you whip your hand back from right to left to form your crossbar. Now, you may think this is efficient because you didn't lift the pen to cross your *t*. But where did you end up? You wound up on the left side of the stem, moving in the wrong direction. This backward stroke, called the "whip stroke," occurs in the scripts of writers who are constantly second-guessing themselves.

The personal pronoun "I" represents how you feel about yourself. A big "I" shows that you feel confident and sure about yourself. A small "I" shows that you feel small and put yourself down. Do you see that your personal pronoun "I" is not much bigger than your lowercase letters?

Knock that little whipping boy off your shoulder. You know the one. The one who keeps saying you "should/would/could have . . ." You've been through some turbulence, for sure. So it may take some time for you to build up your confidence and soar again. Show yourself and the world that you have confidence in yourself by making your personal pronoun "I" big and strong.

And don't forget to make your *t*-bar crossings from left to right. Think "full throttle, forward!" and remember what they say in flight school: "It's always a good idea to keep the pointy end going forward as much as possible."

Anorexia in Her Script

Dear Michelle,

I am a junior in college and I am very concerned about my youngest sister, Dawn. She is 16 years old and wants to be a professional ballet dancer. I know that there is always pressure on her to stay thin. She thinks she is fat even though she probably weighs no more than 80 pounds. When I went home to visit last month a bunch of us piled into the car. I told her to sit on my lap. I figured that she was such a light weight that she would feel like a feather. Instead, the experience was very painful. Her "butt" bones were so sharp that they actually dug into my thighs like a knife.

I am sending you the last letter Dawn wrote me. All she talks about is her weight and how fat she is. Please look at her handwriting. Can you tell if she is anorexic from her handwriting?

Thank you,
Melissa from NYC

Dear Melissa,

Dawn is showing signs, both in her actions and in her handwriting, that she has anorexia nervosa, a serious eating disorder that involves self-starvation. Anorexics like Dawn suffer from low self-worth. They want to whittle away until they disappear.

The personal pronoun "I" represents the self or ego. Look at the way Dawn made her *I*'s. Do you notice how small they are? The size of Dawn's personal pronoun reveals how Dawn perceives herself.

The lower-case *f* stands for food, fat, and full-figured. People who make fat *f*'s are frequently obsessed with food. Dawn makes the bottom of her *f* with an inflated "belly." This doesn't mean that Dawn actually has a protruding belly; it just means that she thinks she does.

Your sister needs to get treatment for her eating disorder immediately.

Love Object

Dear Michelle,

Let me tell you about my situation. About a year ago I became involved with a certain woman who happened to be in a loveless marriage. I was honest with her from the very start and told her that I could offer her only friendship. But, still her feelings for me grew very strong, very quickly.

The feelings were not mutual. Against my better judgment, I continued to let her come around. Now, I believe that she is completely and totally in love with me. She makes it seem as if she can't live without me. I wonder why I just don't end it because she's getting in deeper and deeper.

What's going to happen when I come across a lady whom I really want to be with? It will crush her when I leave her alone.

Am I a friend or a mental case?

Sign me . . . Love Object

her come around. Now I believe she is in complete and total love with me. She makes it seem that she can't live without me. I wonder why I ...

Dear Love Object,

Let me rephrase your question: Are you an innocent "love object" who doesn't want to hurt a vulnerable woman or are you a foot-dragging shloomp (just your average shmo who can't say "no")?

You may not be a true shmo, as far as shmos go, but your handwriting does show that you're, well, a wee bit lazy.

The way a writer crosses his *t*'s shows how he moves forward in life. The stronger and firmer the *t* crossings, the more determined the writer is to push onward.

Take a look at the way you cross your *t*'s, Do you notice that many of your *t*-bars are barely there? Your weak *t* crossings show that you are not moving forward.

You are stringing this woman along because it's easy. You don't have to plan dates, woo her, or even think about a future together. In fact, you don't have to make any decisions at all—at least not yet! But remember, the easy way out in the short run often makes life harder in the long run. Be kind, but make it clear to your lady friend that any romance is out of the picture.

It's time to get a move on it and stop dragging your feet. Set goals, make plans, and take action. Put some oomph into your life and be the kind of man that's worthy of being a love object.

The Jokester

Dear Michelle,

Hi there! I have the distinction of always being the class clown! I am not the shy type! Friends and coworkers frequently ask me for my opinion because they know I will be honest and direct with them. I can be quite loud and am always the jokester and prankster in any group.

Also, as a writer, I am overly self aware of my unusual writing and printing style. What do you think?

Thanks,
The Jokester
Miami, FL

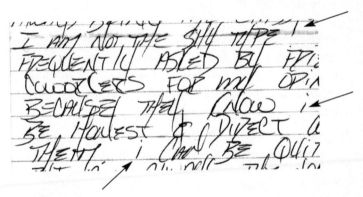

Dear Jokester,

There's an old expression that says clowns are laughing on the outside and crying on the inside.

Let's see what your handwriting says about you "inside."

Your script is unique and large. It demands to be seen. Your large and unusual script says, "Hey there, notice me! Can't you see that I'm big and important?" Also, after many of your sentences you place an exclamation point, when a period would do just fine. Why? Because an exclamation point shouts: "What I'm saying is important! It really is!"

The way a writer makes his personal pronoun "I" shows how he truly feels about himself. Often, you write your personal pronoun with an itty-bitty lowercase *i*, which says, "Oh me, oh my, I'm just a little boy who wants to hide and shrink away."

You use your boisterous behavior to conceal your self-doubt. Perhaps you're afraid that if you say something without hiding behind a joke, people will not listen . . . or care.

Like many successful comedians, you use humor as a defense against low self-esteem. Joan Rivers, for example, would joke about her feelings as an ugly duckling: "I was such a dog, my father had to throw a bone down the aisle just to get me married." Ronnie Shakes declared, "I wouldn't mind being the last man on earth—just to see if all those girls were telling me the truth."

So dear Jokester, don't lose your sense of humor—but work on your self-esteem, starting with your personal pronoun. When your little *i* has become a strong, confident uppercase *I*, you'll feel better about yourself and have the freedom and confidence to let both sides of your personality, humorous and serious, shine through.

Gene Donor Desperately Seeks Willing Recipient

Dear Michelle,

My life has been a roller coaster ride that seems to have no ending. I am a very complicated person with a compassionate heart. I know I have the ability to give so much love to a soul mate.

If I get close to someone I back off because I want to know if she's "the one." I have looked for the right person far and wide.

Two months ago, I saw a girl. The way she moved, the way she talked—she mesmerized me. I am always calling her but I can't get her to call me back. I just can't blank her out of my mind like I do the rest. She may be my angel— God knows I need one.

Please look at my handwriting and tell me what you suggest. I need desperately to pass on my genes to the next generation. I'm 57 and time is of the essence.
Sincerely,
Matthew from Seattle, WA

Dear Matthew,

Fifty-seven is certainly not too old to be a father. Look at Paul McCartney. He became a new father at 61. You say you want to pass on your genes to the next generation. But the question is: Is the next generation ready for your genes? Let's see what your handwriting has to say.

First, look at your *y* in the word "may." Do you see how the bottom loop reaches leftward and ends in a hook? This backwards hook, known as the felon's claw, appears in the handwriting of people who always find themselves in bad situations. Or should I say bad situations always find them? Deep down, felon's claw writers feel guilty (guilty about what . . . who knows?). But, their deep-rooted guilt leads them to make decisions that will get them what they feel they deserve: to be punished. So I'm not at all surprised that your life has been one big roller coaster ride.

Also notice how you wrote the word "angel." Do you see how the *A* and the *N* are capitalized, but the *g, e, l* are lower case? When capital letters pop up irregularly throughout a script, it shows that the writer is unpredictable.

Before you start swimming in that gene pool, Matthew, you need to get yourself unmesmerized and uncomplicated, not to mention situated and stable. Let's face it, few women want their baby's papa to be a human roller coaster—a Rolling Stone, maybe, but that's another story.

The Dating Game

Dear Michelle,

I am wondering if maybe you can give me some insight as to why I cannot seem to find the right guy. I have been single for five years, am 36, am pretty, slim, and have a nice house & nice career. I have three children ages 9, 11 & 13 but they don't seem a hindrance in date proposals. There are always guys interested in dating me.

I have only been on a handful of dates, none of which progressed past the third date. No one seems to interest me yet I do want to find a partner.

I do have to admit to being very selective. I want to find the right guy & most who ask me out are unsuitable for my lifestyle. I have to believe that the right man is out there somewhere. I never dreamed it would be so hard.

Lonely in Tampa

Dear Lonely,

Infatuation is when you think he's as sexy as Paul Newman, as smart as Albert Einstein, as noble as a monk, as rich as Bill Gates, as funny as Woody Allen, and is built like a Chippendale's dancer. Love is when you realize he's as sexy as Woody Allen, as rich as a monk, as funny as Bill Gates, as smart as a Chippendale's dancer, is built like Albert Einstein, and is nothing like Paul Newman, but you'll take him anyway. What kind of man could win your hand? Let's look at your handwriting. Notice the words "house," "have," "hindrance," and "proposals." They begin with a long, rounded lead-in stroke, which resembles a cupped hand. This outstretched hand says: "Hey, baby, fill me with nice pretty things—maybe something small like a chocolate, or a diamond, or perhaps the keys to a Mercedes."

Before you date the next guy, take a good look at his handwriting. You need a Mr. Right who can take care of you in the lifestyle to which you'd like become accustomed. The handwriting of a take-charge, high-powered man will typically go uphill and slant slightly to the right. His *t*-bars will be high and strong, indicating lofty goals and the strength to achieve them. You'll definitely want your man to be generous. So look for cupped-hand strokes at the ends of his words. This shows that his hands are open to give.

But handwriting is only part of the story. You'll know you've found your Mr. Right when one day, he takes your hand in his and suddenly, your head becomes dizzy, your heart begins to pound, and you feel like you're walking on air. Of course, this could also mean that you're coming down with the flu!

Who Loves You, Baby?

Dear Michelle,

Enclosed is the handwriting of eight girls. I am sending you these letters and cards to figure out which of these girls love me or don't love me. What else can you tell me about them? Should I write back to all of them or get rid of some of them?

Thank you,
J.B., San Diego, CA

Gal #1

d me a bit. Well I,m going to close
I,ll hear from you soon, take care

Gal #2

And I lied, I did Send you underwear,
Just to Remind you the "good girl" you left

Gal #3

Dear J.B.,

Let's take a look at the handwriting of three of the gals.

Gal #1 begins her letter with, "Dear Baby Boy," and ends with "Don't make me hurt you, Baby. Then again, I probably will. You know you enjoy pain. Love Bad Baby Girl." My first clue that gal #1 might be more than a tad strange is her doodle on the top of the page. While other gals decorate their cards with hearts and flowers, this Bad Baby Girl's doodles include vomit, doggie-doo, and a ribbon-adorned skull surrounded by flames.

Gal #2 writes: "Here's the bad news. I went out, met a guy. Anyways, we had a fling as one does. Needless to say, I am pregnant again. I do not know what else to say, I am not seeing this guy, I am not in love with him. I,m going to close now, hopefully, I,ll hear from you soon, take care of yourself." Gal #2 places commas where there should be apostrophes, periods where there should be commas, and commas where there should be periods. Gal #2's topsy-turvy punctuation tells me she's a bit discombobulated.

And finally, gal #3 writes, "And I lied, I did send you underwear, just to remind you of the 'good girl' you left behind." Hmm . . . if her underwear is as teeny as her writing it would sure save on postage. Often, teeny writing is a sign of shyness. But gal #3's writing also shows she has a wild side. She mixes capital letters unpredictably with lower-case letters. Look at the two different *r*'s in the word "underwear." When you least expect it, this shy librarian will become Zelda the lion tamer!

Who loves you, baby? Heck, they're all crazy about you. Who should you write back to? I suppose that all depends on you. Is your dream gal a darkly dangerous "Bad Baby Girl," a discombobulated pregnant rule breaker, or a "good girl" with a wild side and bare behind? Be sure to keep me posted, OK?

Jailhouse Blues

Dear Michelle,

I am writing to you from San Quentin Prison. I am writing to you because I am curious about what you can possibly tell me about myself from my handwriting.

Is it good or is it bad? I really would like to know the extent of it.

I also would like to know if my handwriting has anything to do with me not having a sincere pen pal to correspond with. Or is it simply my preference that continues to stand in my way?

All I ever require is the woman be a god fearing Christian, single, childless, drug free, cigarette free, and alcohol free. But for some reason I can't seem to connect with that kind of woman.

I've been incarcerated now for 20 years, and I've corre-

sponded with many women, but not one of them turned out to be the angel in my dreams. Why me?

I guess you will give me a clue after you analyze my handwriting.

Sincerely, Tony

Dear Tony,

Your handwriting is neat, even, and perfect—too perfect! What does this mean? It means that you try very hard to make things in your life look perfect. You have learned to cover up your true self and hide behind the flawless image that you have created.

Your overly controlled script also shows that, deep down, you have a fear of losing control.

You expect a lot from yourself and your pen pals—too much.

Face it, Tony, you're not perfect. Perfect men don't spend twenty years in prison searching for a perfect pen pal. Learn to accept people's imperfections and differences, including your own. And remember, the only place you'll find the perfect "angel of your dreams" is when you're fast asleep.

Sleepy Head

Dear Michelle,

I don't know if you can help me or not, but here goes, I have a problem with getting up on time in the morning. Every night I tell myself that I'll wake up when my alarm goes off at six AM but I always snooze an extra hour.

Do you have any suggestions?
        Thanks, Sleepy Head in Columbia, S.C.

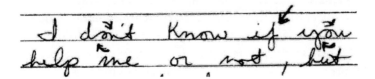

Dear Sleepy Head,

I do know one sure-fire solution to your problem: put a mousetrap on top of your alarm clock. That'll keep you from going back to sleep!

But since I'm sure you'd prefer to keep all your fingers, let's see if your handwriting suggests a better solution. The upper zone (the upper loops of the letters *b, d, f, h, k, l,* and *t*) represents what's happening in our heads, like thinking, planning, and feeling. The lower zone (the lower loops of the letters *f, g, j, p, q,* and *y*) represents what's happening in our bodies, or the physical actions we take. The letter *f* is the only letter in our alphabet that has both an upper zone and a lower zone. A well-balanced *f* is a sign of an organized person. By "well-balanced," I mean that the writer's *f* is formed with upper and lower loops that are the same size and are joined at the center point between the two loops.

Notice that the upper and lower loops of your *f*'s are not balanced. Most your upper loops are much narrower and smaller than your lower loops, indicating that you are not the world's most organized person. So I would suggest that if you want to wake up an hour earlier, try to be more organized so that you can get to bed an hour earlier!

But there's something else going on in your handwriting. Look very carefully at your *o*'s. Do you see how you make your circles backwards from right to left instead of left to right? This underhanded *o* shows that you have a tendency to "trick" yourself and others. I wouldn't be surprised if you were doing things to sabotage yourself so that you can't get up in the mornings.

Don't give in to your little tricks. Put yourself on a very organized time schedule. And write your *f*'s with upper and lower loops that are balanced and joined in the middle.

If all else fails, here is a perfect excuse to give your boss: A recent study has revealed that getting more sleep can improve a person's brainpower and creativity!

The Princess and the Pervert

Dear Michelle,

Hi there. I've been unhappily married for 5 years. Before I married my husband, he treated me like a princess. He was very kind, respectful, always there when I needed him. He really treated me great. After we got married and I got pregnant everything changed 360 degrees. The good man I knew, switched into a very bad, mean, crazy person.

Most of the time he spends in his computer room surfing adult web pages. I even caught him several times staring at naked women on the monitor and these women were showing a close up of their lower private parts. Sad to say, my husband was really enjoying it.

He beats me. Later, when bruises appear, he asks where I got the bruises. When I tell him it's from where he punched and kicked me, he denies it.

I asked him to go with me to see a psychiatrist for marriage counseling. But, he told me he wouldn't go to counseling because counseling is only for sick people.

I've had 5 years of misery. I'm really confused of what to do. I'm really scared and bothered with my situation. What is wrong with him? Is it time for me to move on . . . maybe give him what he wants . . . DIVORCE. I am attaching a copy of his handwriting. Please help me.

Respectfully yours, Martyr Wife, Baton Rouge, LA

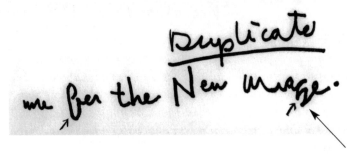

Dear Martyr Wife,

The lower zone (the lower loops of the letters *f, g, j, p, q,* and *y*) represents our sexual drives and desires. Look at the way your husband made his *g* in the word "image."

Instead of a normal, rounded lower loop, he has a sharp, angular, stroke that thrusts to the right. The absence of loops in his lower zone shows he cares zip about a normal, caring, loving, sexual relationship with a "real" woman.

Also, notice the bizarre shape of the *g* in "image." While he normally writes without any lower zone to speak of, occasionally, an "appendage" appears in his middle zone, where it shouldn't normally be. This is a sign of a man with bizarre sexual habits.

And speaking of appendages, do you see how his *f* in the word "for" resembles a certain male appendage? This is almost always a sign of a writer with unusual sexual fantasies and habits.

You asked me if you should move on. Well, if I were married to a "very bad, mean, crazy person" who was addicted to porn and beat me, I'd run so fast that lightning wouldn't catch me.

Why do you stay? You typed your question to me. Write me back with a handwritten letter, and I'll let you know why you have molasses under your feet.

Three's a Crowd

Dear Michelle,

I am divorced for two years and have been living with my ex-husband for one year. He has another woman he works with and goes out with. He has recently told me he loves both of us. This whole situation is driving me crazy. I still love him but I can't keep on staying with him with her in the picture.

He has been seeing this woman for two years. He says he doesn't ever want to get married again. To me or to her. Can you give me some insights from my handwriting?

Sign me "Used and Confused"

Dear Used and Confused,

How can you tell if your man is playing around? He sends you love notes that are photocopied and begin with the line "To whom it may concern . . ."

You've acknowledged that your man is unfaithful. So why do you stay? Do you believe that he'll wake up tomorrow and be a different man? That he'll give up all other women and commit to you? That he'll suddenly realize that you're the hottest tamale this side of the Rio Grande?

The height of a writer's *t*-crossings represents the height of their goals and dreams. All I had to do is take one look at the way you crossed your *t*'s to know that you are a dreamer. Many of your *t*'s are crossed so high that the cross-bar is detached and floats above the stem. Like your floating cross-bars, your head can get lost in the clouds. You become a dreamer, detached from reality. You see your man as you wish he would be: your knight in shining armor. But can you accept him for who he really is: a two-timing, double-dealing, highfalutin, ego-tooting, noncommitting, good-for-nothing . . . roommate?

As W. C. Fields said: "If at first you don't succeed, try, try, again. Then quit. No use being a damn fool."

Have courage to let go of the things not worth sticking to.

So if you want to uncover the truth, the whole truth and nothing but the truth, take another look at the evidence all around you: the writing on that birthday card or love letter, the note scribbled on a crumpled sheet of paper in the trash, those doodles in a notebook, that shopping list on your refrigerator door . . .

RESOURCES

Bird, Anne. *Blood Brother: 33 Reasons My Brother Scott Peterson Is Guilty.* New York: HarperCollins, 2005.

Cornwell, Patricia. *Portrait of a Killer: Jack the Ripper—Case Closed.* New York: Berkley True Crime, 2003.

Douglas, John, and Mark Olshaker. *The Cases That Haunt Us: From Jack the Ripper to JonBenét Ramsey, the FBI's Legendary Mindhunter Sheds Light on the Mysteries that Won't Go Away.* New York: Scribner, 2000.

Evans, Stewart P., and Paul Gainey. *Jack the Ripper: First American Serial Killer.* New York: Kodansha America, 1998.

Evans, Stewart P., and Keith Skinner. *Jack the Ripper: Letters from Hell.* London: Sutton, 2005.

———. *The Ultimate Jack the Ripper Companion.* New York: Carroll & Graf, 2000.

Hubbard, L. Ron. Quoted in Russell Miller, *Bare-Faced Messiah: The True Story of L. Ron Hubbard.* London: Penguin Books, 1987, pp. 247–49.

Ianetta, Kimon, Reed Hayes, et al. *Danger Between the Lines: Facilitating Assessment of Dangerousness Using Handwriting Characteristics.* Kailua, HI: Kimon Ianetta, 1993.

Larson, Erik. *The Devil in the White City: Murder, Magic, and Madness at the Fair that Changed America.* New York: Crown Publishers, 2003.

McNichol, Andrea, and Jeffrey A. Nelson. *Handwriting Analysis: Putting It to Work for You.* Chicago: Contemporary Books, 1994

National Archives. Letter written by Fidel Castro in 1940 (at the age of 14) to President Roosevelt. Item from Record Group 84: Records of the Foreign Service Posts of the Department of State, 1788–1964, 1940

Correspondence, Part 12, 800-800.1, Civilian Records LICON, Tex-
tual Archives Services Division (NWCTC), National Archives at College Park, 8601 Adelphi Road, College Park, MD 20740-6001
[Online version at http://arcweb.archives.gov/arc/]

Olsen, Gregg. *Starvation Heights.* New York: Warner Books, 1997.

Owen, David. *Hidden Evidence: Forty True Crimes and How Forensic Science Helped Solve Them.* New York: Firefly Books Ltd., 2000.

Posner, Gerald. Quoted from PBS/*Frontline*'s Web-exclusive companion to
the rebroadcast of the 1993 documentary *Who Was Lee Harvey
Oswald?* http://www.pbs.org/wgbh/pages/frontline/shows/oswald/
forum/.

Sanford, David. *Me & Ralph: Is Nader Unsafe for America?* Washington,
D.C.: New Republic Book Company, 1976.

Stewart, James B. *Blind Eye.* New York: Touchstone, 1999.

Walker, Kent, with Mark Schone. *Son of a Grifter: The Twisted Tale of Sante
and Kenny Kimes, the Most Notorious Con Artists in America.* New
York: HarperCollins, 2001.

Watts, Michael. *Love-Script: What Handwriting Reveals About Love and
Sexuality.* New York: St. Martin's Griffin, 1995.

Wolf v. Ramsey and Ramsey (Robert Christian Wolf, Plaintiff v. John Benét
Ramsey & Patricia Paugh Ramsey, Defendants), Civil Action File
No. 00-CIV-1187 (JEC), United States District Court, Northern District of Georgia, Atlanta Division. Letter and word samples used in the
author's analysis of Patsy Ramsey's handwriting (Chapter 18) were
extracted from charts created by Cina Wong, a handwriting analyst
hired in that case, that are included in Exhibit B to "Plaintiff's
Response to the City of Boulder's Motion for a Protective Order,"
(submitted 18 February, 2003).

ACKNOWLEDGMENTS

Thank you, Agnes Birnbaum, for being the best agent, ever.

Thank you, Liz Stein, for your clear vision and insightful editing.

Thank you, Joel, my amazing brother, for your patient guidance inside and outside the courtroom.

Thank you, Cherie, my extraordinary sister, for introducing me to handwriting analysis.

Thank you, Dorothy, my super mother, for encouraging my creative side. (Can you believe it? I finished the book!)

Thank you, Hank, for making my mother happy.

Thank you, Ziggy Maggoo, for staying by my feet and keeping me company while I was writing.

Thank you, Janet Martha, for your helpful research.

Thank you, Ron Freeman, for believing in me.

Thank you, Robert Wechsler, for your constructive critique.

Thank you, Maris Kreizman, for keeping Jim and me on schedule.

Thank you, Erich Hobbing, for your heroic design work.

Thank you, family and friends, for your counsel and support. That includes you Marilyn, Amy, Geoffrey, Fred, Barbara, Dair, Tim, Rege, Judy and James.

Thank you, Jim Kwalwasser, my coauthor and best friend. I couldn't have done it without you.

ABOUT THE AUTHOR

Michelle Dresbold has been called the Sherlock Holmes of handwriting. For the past ten years, she has been helping law enforcement agencies around the country put away the "bad guys."

A graduate of the United States Secret Service's Advanced Document Examination training program, Michelle consults to private attorneys, police departments, and prosecutors throughout the United States. She is considered one of the top experts in the nation on handwriting identification (including anonymous letters and suspected forgeries), personality profiling, and threat analysis. She has testified in a wide variety of cases including arson, embezzlement, voting fraud, forgery, stalking, and murder.

She is the author of the syndicated column "The Handwriting Doctor," where she uses her skills as a handwriting profiler to diagnose and address a variety of problems. Michelle is also an accomplished artist, who has shown her work in galleries and museums across the country. She graduated with high honors from the University of Michigan, with a degree in fine arts and psychology.

James Kwalwasser is an editor and writer who lives in Pittsburgh. He is the cocreator and editor of "The Handwriting Doctor" syndicated column.